AFRICA

THE POLITICS OF
INDEPENDENCE

AFRICA
THE POLITICS OF INDEPENDENCE

*An Interpretation
of Modern African History*

BY

IMMANUEL WALLERSTEIN

VINTAGE BOOKS

A Division of Random House

NEW YORK

To Ruth

AND

To the young people of Africa
who are forging their future as they deem wise
and who thereby merit our respect

Copyright© 1961, 1971, by Immanuel Wallerstein

All rights reserved under
International and Pan-American Copyright Conventions.
Published in the United States by Random House, Inc.,
New York, and simultaneously in Canada
by Random House of Canada Limited, Toronto.
Originally published by Vintage Books,
a division of Random House, Inc.,
in 1961.

ISBN: 0-394-70206-9
Library of Congress Catalog Card Number: 61-16964
MANUFACTURED IN THE UNITED STATES OF AMERICA

Vintage Books Edition, November 1961

CONTENTS

Introduction   3

I · Africa Before the Europeans Came   11

THE COLONIAL ERA

II · The Social Change   29

III · The Reaction   45

IV · The Different European Legacies   63

INDEPENDENCE AND AFTER

V · Internal Unity: Parties and Heroes   85

VI · Larger Unities: Pan-Africanism and
      Regional Federations   103

VII · Cultural Revival   121

VIII · Africa and the World   137

IX · Prospects for Democracy   153

Maps   9, 83

Epilogue   169

Appendix   176

Bibliographical Note   178

Index   follows page 180

ACKNOWLEDGMENTS

Acknowledgments should really start with those who have contributed most to the author's understanding. In my case, this is a group of people—friends and acquaintances—who have been part of the process of social change, the rise of nationalism, the building of new nations described in this book. What I learned most from them, from wherever they have come, has been the similarity of themes—the frustrations and hopes, the uncertainties and self-assurance—which they all, in varying degrees, display. I am grateful that they enriched my world and my appreciation of my own culture by allowing me closer access to theirs.

My friends and colleagues, Professors A. Etzioni, T. K. Hopkins, and R. Schachter, read the manuscript and gave me valuable advice, but, as usual, bear none of the blame.

AFRICA

THE POLITICS OF
INDEPENDENCE

"The wind of change is blowing through [Africa], and whether we like it or not this growth of national consciousness is a political fact. We must all accept it as a fact, and our national policies must take account of it."   Prime Minister Harold Macmillan
Speech to Houses of Parliament of the
Union of South Africa
February 3, 1960

"It is not Africa which should be asked whether it belongs to one camp or another; it is rather to the two camps, to the East and to the West, that we must put the question which we consider as fundamental and of paramount importance: Yes or no, are you for the liberation of Africa?"   President Sékou Touré
Address to General Assembly of
the United Nations
November 5, 1959

>Dark Africa?
>Who nursed the doubtful child
>Of civilization
>On the wand'ring banks
>Of life-giving Nile,
>And gave to the teeming nations
>Of the West
>A Grecian gift!
>>From the poem, *"Africa Speaks"*
>>by Michael Dei-Anang

INTRODUCTION

The rapid political developments in Africa in the last five years have made Africa a familiar subject to the reader of newspapers and magazines. The early personal accounts of European travelers, missionaries and administrators have ceded place both to an ever-increasing number of serious monographs by scholars and to surveys and compendia, many of which unfortunately, and perhaps inevitably, become outdated almost as quickly as they are published.

This book is neither an account of travel nor a monograph nor a survey. It is an interpretative essay that seeks to place within an overall perspective the whole range of modern political developments on the African continent. I have hoped to assist the general reader in understanding the day-by-day developments in African countries by enabling him to fit the confusing array of men and events into the framework of general patterns.

For the serious student of African affairs and of political sociology, I have tried to use the empirical analysis of recent African history to throw some light on general propositions. In particular, I have been interested in two central questions in the analysis of society.

First of all, I have been concerned with the ways in which social structures—in this case, colonial administrations—generate within themselves social conflict, and under what conditions this social conflict results in a revolution which overthrows the structure. This question is dealt with primarily in Chapters II–IV on the colonial era.

Secondly, I have been concerned with the ways in which social structures, especially new ones—in this case, the independent African states—hold themselves together, acquire the loyalty of their subjects in a complex economy where the interests of the citizens vary widely. These questions are dealt with in various ways in Chapters V–IX.

Throughout both parts of the book, I have asked the questions: To whom are political allegiances owed? What makes men shift their allegiances from one group to another, from one set of rules to another? How can some men get others to shift their allegiances? In the process of shifting allegiances, what causes resistance and what facilitates the shift? Finally, how can shifts of allegiances be made relatively durable?

These are primarily political questions, then, with which I am concerned. This does not mean that economic factors are unimportant or negligible. This does mean that the focus of this essay will be on the political structures, on the levers of power, including the ideologies of both rulers and dissenters. Purely economic questions such as the natural resources of Africa, the ways in which these resources might most rapidly be developed, and the monetary policies of the new African states will not be considered, except insofar as they reflect or are an integral part of the political process. This is, of course, an extremely difficult line to draw, perhaps an arbitrary one. However, the major concerns of this essay have now been indicated, and the reader

will expect that the material to be included has been
selected on the basis of its relevance to these major
concerns.

This essay, furthermore, in two senses does not pre-
tend to be complete. It will not give the reader much of
the story of the developments in any particular African
country, and it will give him only to a limited extent
the modern political history of the African continent as
a whole. This essay attempts only to put forward some
hypotheses, to indicate their connections with each
other, and to give some suggestive evidence based on
African political history. The general statements will
usually be illustrated by specific examples, but these
examples are not intended to be exhaustive. The essay,
in other words, does not provide definitive evidence in
favor of its hypotheses. For this, a longer work, based
probably on a wider geographical base and certainly
requiring much empirical research not yet done, would
have to be undertaken.

There are two warnings the reader would do well to
bear in mind. First, because the purpose of the essay is
twofold—to indicate what is going on in Africa, and to
analyze some more general social processes—the statements are of two sorts. There are some which concern a
single entity, the African continent, and are necessarily
descriptive and historical. This is true, for example, of
Chapter I, which tells the pre-European history of
Africa, and of part of the discussion of the history of
pan-Africanism in modern times. Other statements,
probably the majority, use as the unit under discussion
the African colony or independent state, of which there
are several dozen. These statements are generalizations,
true of the large majority. Where there are important
exceptions to the rule, they are usually indicated.

This brings us to the second warning. There are some
standard exceptions that should be made in advance.
Liberia and Ethiopia were at practically no point in
the modern era under European colonial rule. There-

fore, while certain general statements about the effects of urbanization and modernization apply, neither country knew a colonial administration, and consequently neither saw the rise of a nationalist movement to gain its independence. Many of the generalizations, therefore, do not apply to these so-called "old independent states." Furthermore, Libya obtained its independence in 1950 not because of internal developments but because Italy lost the Second World War, and the victors agreed on Libya's independence as the best way of minimizing each other's role in Libya's future. Many statements, therefore, do not apply to Libya.

Most of the statements in Chapters V–IX apply only to *independent* African nations, but not to the Republic of South Africa,* where a white settler minority rules. As of the writing of this book, it seems likely that the remaining nonindependent states of Africa will become independent within several years. It is my expectation that the problems these new states will face and the manner in which they will face them will not differ substantially from what we have seen heretofore in those African states presently independent.

Lastly, it has been my decision to include within the scope of this book all of Africa, as defined by the physical geographers. The size of the appropriate group about which to generalize has itself been a matter of considerable debate among scholars and politicians. Some write about Tropical Africa from the Sahara to the Limpopo River, thus excluding Arab North Africa and the Republic of South Africa. Others write about Africa South of the Sahara, thus excluding only the North. And some write about Africa. The reasons for my choice for this book will, I trust, become clear to the reader in the arguments of the essay itself.

The interpretation of contemporary history is im-

* Known until July 1, 1961 as the Union of South Africa.

portant for those who wish to advance knowledge in the social sciences because much more extensive and controllable data is available here than from the study of past history. But it is equally important for men who wish to understand their world in order to act upon it. These two tasks are not separable ones. For if knowledge may be distorted when we try to adapt it to the needs of contemporary man, it nevertheless finds its ultimate justification in aiding him rationally to determine the ways to his own betterment. This essay seeks to contribute to both tasks simultaneously.

PRECOLONIAL AFRICA
*(Arrows indicate some principal routes
of migration, conquest, and trade)*

: I :

AFRICA BEFORE

THE EUROPEANS CAME

Africa has greatness in her past as well as her present. In the past, the history of the world has often been written as though it were the history of Europe, including its precursors and its extensions. Of all the areas of the world, Africa has been the most neglected by historians, who have indeed often denied that there was any history in Africa to study. As late as 1951, a British historian wrote: "Until the very recent penetration by Europe the greater part of the [African] continent was without the wheel, the plough and the transport animal, almost without stone houses or clothes except for skins; without writing and so without history."

Without writing and so without history—this was the theme. Yet it is not true that there was no writing; and even if it were, it would not then follow that there was no history. For history exists wherever man exists, and the history of the peoples of Africa has been one of variety and invention, of skills in art and government. It is a history at least as old as that of Europe, at least as interesting if less known, and some would argue as impressive.

This book is not concerned with all of African history.

It is an interpretation of *modern* African history—how European colonial rule abetted the process of modernization and nurtured nationalism; and how African nations, having regained their independence from Europe, are seeking to further the process of modernization. Yet, in order to appreciate modern Africa adequately, we should start by taking a brief look at Africa before the Europeans came. We do this for two reasons. First, the reader ought to be aware that Africa does indeed have a history, one to which contemporary nationalists make increasing reference, as we shall see. Second, in some ways, the facts of pre-European history partially determine the patterns of modern Africa. The reader may thus find it helpful to know the ancient historical elements that lie behind some aspects of modern African politics. This chapter serves as a rapid survey of Africa's pre-European history.

A history of Africa must start with Egypt. I say "must," although a few years ago many writers would have argued that Egypt was part of a Middle Eastern world, a cradle of Western civilization. But in these last few years, some Africans have sought to reclaim Egypt for Africa and to assert that the ancient Egyptians, builders of temples and of monuments, scientists and religious thinkers, were Negroes. That this question is a matter of scholarly debate is an important reflection of contemporary African history. That Egyptian civilization, be it white or Negro or both, made its influence felt southward into Africa as well as northward into Europe is an important base line for the study of ancient African history.

It perhaps would not matter who the Egyptians were, had such an issue not been made of it during the period of European colonization. As we shall see later, the nonexistence of Negro achievements was fundamental to colonial ideology, which attempted to attribute all signs of human accomplishment to Egyptians, or Hittites, or Phoenicians, or Arabs, or Hamites, and

never to Negroes. It was assumed, or implied, or indeed
on occasion boldly asserted that Egyptians or Hittites
or Phoenicians or Arabs or Hamites were white men,
or at least whiter men than the Negroes. We shall return
to this issue later in the context of colonialism and
nationalism. Suffice it to say now, for the purpose of
discussing the African past, that the best evidence of
today seems to indicate a very great racial intermin-
gling, in Africa as elsewhere, over the past five thousand years, and that the "Egyptians" or "Hamites" of
yesteryear might well find themselves classified as
Negroes today, in precisely those countries where such
classifications matter. Suffice it further to note that
many of the archaeological remains of which we shall
speak, at first credited to "Arabs" or "Hamites," have
on closer, or less biased, inspection, turned out to be
unmistakably Negro-African in origin.

But let us return to Egypt. As the Egyptians turned
south, they came upon a people called the Kushites,
who seem to have inhabited what is now southern
Egypt and the northern part of the Sudan somewhere
between 800 B.C. and 300 A.D. Their early center,
Napata, gave way in the sixth century B.C. to Meroë.
The ruins of Meroë, which are quite extensive, show
the flourishing of a Bronze Age. Meroë became a center
for the smelting and the manufacture of iron. Our records concerning Meroë are hieroglyphs not yet deciph-
ered, but it is clear that Meroë was a major African
center of its time, and that its contributions were not
only in the fields of manufacture and trade but as a
center for the exchange of ideas, of religious concepts,
of technical knowledge.

It may be that Meroë provides the historical link
between Egyptian culture and the peoples of the Western Sudan,* which so much legend and harder evidence

* The Western Sudan is not the western half of the Republic of
the Sudan, formerly called the Anglo-Egyptian Sudan; it is an
area in West Africa on the same latitude as the Sudan. Largely

seems to argue existed. Was the use of iron first brought
to Chad and Nigeria from Meroë, or did it come down
from Libya? We are not yet sure. We do know that
there were important waves of migration westward
from the region of Meroë to the Western Sudan. This
migration went on over a period of centuries, maybe
longer, and established a trans-African route eastward
which is still used today by African Moslems, making
the pilgrimage of piety to Mecca.

Further west in the Sahara, on the rocks and in the
canyons of the Tassili Mountains, paintings have been
discovered which show Egyptian-style boats and two-
wheeled chariots. And such rock paintings are being
discovered straight southward across the Sahara. These
naturalistic portraits, painted by ancient Negro peoples,
seem to date back beyond 3000 B.C. And in Nigeria we
have today many terra-cotta heads of great artistry
which date at least to 900 B.C. This is the "Nok"
culture.

At the same period of time that Meroë flourished, the
city of Carthage in North Africa was born and grew to
challenge Rome, and ultimately to be defeated. This
story has perhaps been better known than that of
Meroë. Carthage seems to have existed since the ninth
century B.C. and to have conquered much of the rest of
what is today Tunisia about the fifth century B.C.

During the early period, Carthage not only pushed
forward into Europe through Spain but made contact
through the Libyan desert with Garamantes, in what
is today called the Fezzan (southern Libya). It is
thought that caravans took thirty days to make the
journey, and that the people of Garamantes may themselves have engaged in trade with the Western Sudan.

Carthage was of course conquered by Rome. And
Rome proceeded to "Romanize" North Africa, as later

grasslands merging into desert, it includes the present-day re-
publics of Mauritania, Mali, Upper Volta, Niger, Chad, and the
Northern Region of Nigeria.

Europe would seek to "Westernize" all of Africa. Christianity, too, spread along with Roman power, although the Christian missionaries of those days were not, at least at first, related to the imperial power in the same way as the Christian missionaries of a later era.

The collapse of the Roman empire in the West brought the Vandals to Morocco in the fifth century A.D. And the slow disintegration of Byzantium permitted the Arab conquest of North Africa in the seventh century.

The Arab empire in its turn began to splinter, allowing once again the beginnings of autonomous states, some say the resurgence of anarchy, in North Africa. During this period of Arab conquest, and even before, there existed in the Western Sudan the first (as far as we know today) of its great Negro empires. We know comparatively little about any earlier period in West Africa because we have as yet discovered no relevant written documents. But the great period of the Western Sudan, the era of its medieval kingdoms, has fortunately had its chroniclers, who wrote mostly in Arabic. The oldest document is by Wahb Ibn Munabbeh and was written in 738 A.D. But the two most important sources are the *Tarikh-es-Sudan*, written around 1655 by Abderrahman es Sadi of Timbuktu, an African of the Fulani people, and the *Tarikh-es-Fettach*, written about 1600 by Mahmoud Kati, also a Negro of Timbuktu. In addition we have the testimony of that great fourteenth-century Arab traveler, Ibn Battuta, and a sixteenth-century African Christian convert, Leo Africanus. It is a serious commentary on European provincialism and the state of medieval Europe's knowledge of its world that though the kingdoms of the Western Sudan began in 400 A.D., Europeans seem to have remained unaware of their history or even their existence until 1400, a gap of a thousand years. Once Europe heard of them, Europeans began to glorify their wealth and exotic qualities. It is from this period that the perhaps exaggerated legends of Timbuktu originate. The disillusionment of nineteenth-century European travelers with this region is in part a function of the illusion their European ancestors were responsible for creating.

The kingdoms of the Western Sudan—Ghana, Mali, Songhay—were remarkable in the degree to which they were able to establish complex political structures that centralized the government of large areas of West Africa. Political superiority here, as often elsewhere, was based on a technological advantage. The ancient empire of Ghana, which was probably founded about 300 A.D., could conquer its neighbors because it knew the use of iron. But having built an empire by their weapons, the people of Ghana maintained it by trade and tribute. For ancient Ghana lay at an important crossroads, between the salt deposits to the north and the gold deposits to the south. Ghana sought, with increasing success, to dominate both resources and monopolize the trade in them. The empire of Ghana stimulated and maintained the flow of trade at a period when the economy of Western Europe was particularly stagnant, the period known as the "Dark Ages."

Toward the eleventh century, a group of Negro Moslems, living in a monastery at the mouth of the Senegal River, created a purified and disciplined version of Islam. These men were called the Almoravids and, under their impulsion, tribes of veiled nomads and blacks rode north and established a new dynasty in Morocco that has survived until today. The Almoravids were crusading warriors of Islam and in 1054 came south again from Morocco. By 1076, they had conquered the capital of Ghana, thus ending the flourishing trade. The political structure of Ghana collapsed.

Indeed the very cities disappeared and the population was to some extent scattered. In recent years some men have argued that the Akan peoples of present-day

Ghana, a thousand miles to the southeast, are the descendants of the inhabitants of ancient Ghana, who migrated south before advancing hostile peoples.

During the thirteenth century, in approximately the same area, a new empire arose, that of Mali or Melle. Sundiata Keita overthrew the rulers of Ghana, then much in decline, and founded a new dynasty. The emperors of Mali were Moslems, and their reign saw the further spread of Islam in West Africa. Mali was not the only centralizing state in the area. There were many principalities and aspiring empires, and there was a constant back-and-forth of conquest and reconquest. What distinguished Mali was its superior skill in the steady organization of centralizing power. Mali was renowned for the extent of its trade, the success of its warfare, the expanding use of metals in war and industry. It utilized currencies of gold or copper or shells.

When the Emperor Mansa Musa made a pilgrimage to Mecca in 1324, he was said to have been accompanied by 60,000 persons and 12,000 slaves dressed in brocade and pure silk. To dispense the alms expected of the pilgrim, the emperor brought with him eighty loads of gold. It is told that every Friday he stopped his caravan and built a mosque. On his return from Mecca, he brought with him a Spanish architect to build him splendid palaces.

Mali's cities, Timbuktu and Djenné, were the focal centers of a wide network of caravans coming from all points of the horizon. We know, for example, that by 1400 the caravans crossing the Sahara to Mali by one of six routes during one year included over 12,000 camels. If the pilgrimage to Mecca was not a common phenomenon, neither was it a rare one. Especially did the professors of the various Moslem seats of learning travel, and thus it was that Timbuktu exchanged learned men with Cordoba.

The Moslem empire of Mali was challenged in the fifteenth century by the Songhay people, rulers of a

small Moslem state, whose capital was Gao. Songhay
was to become the largest kingdom of them all. At its
apogee, Songhay was perhaps the size of the continental
United States, perhaps five times the size of the Holy
Roman Empire at its largest. It covered all the Western
Sudan from what is today Rio de Oro to Chad. It
reached south as far as the forest line. It could go no
further because its power depended on horses. It extended north well into present-day Algeria and Tunisia.
It covered southwest Libya, almost reaching the
Mediterranean near Benghazi.

Islam deserves at least as much credit as a factor in
this extensive political unification as Christianity does
for the Holy Roman Empire. Founded in the eleventh
century, Songhay was made by Sonni Ali in 1464 the
most powerful kingdom in the Western Sudan. Following him was Songhay's most famous ruler, Askia the
Great, who rose to power in 1493. It was in the regime
of Askia the Great that the boundaries of Songhay
reached their greatest extent. He was responsible for
establishing an administrative network that ensured
control of the wide-flung empire. When he made his
pilgrimage to Mecca, Askia the Great was perhaps less
lavish in alms and retinue than Mansa Musa, but he
included many more scholars, so as to enlarge their
knowledge. The University of Sankoré in Timbuktu
became the center of Muslim learning in Africa, but it
was only one of several universities. The practice of
medicine was much advanced, and doctors performed
some operations that were not known in Europe for
another 250 years. Knowledge of Arabic science and
literature was extensive.

Yet once again, armies from Morocco were to descend
and, this time by the use of muskets, destroy an empire.
In 1591 Songhay was defeated and by 1600 the empire
of Songhay was no more. As has happened often in history, not only were men and political structures destroyed, but books and treasures of learning. Never

again—until perhaps tomorrow?—was an empire like
that of Songhay to arise in the Western Sudan. There
would be smaller efforts in the eighteenth and nineteenth centuries—the Fulani emirates of Northern
Nigeria, the Mandingo conquests of Samory—but
these later attempts were to be circumscribed by a new
factor in West African politics, the armies of colonial
Europe.

As we move south into the forest regions of Africa,
we know less of what happened in history. There are no
Arabic documents going back before the fifteenth century. It is only with the arrival of the Portuguese along
the coast at this time that we have written documents,
and their reliability is limited by the fact that European
travelers in Africa at first restricted themselves to a few
port areas and relied on second-hand reports for information about the interior. Furthermore, forest soil is
often unconducive to the preservation of the objects
which archaeologists later seek to find.

Forests are not as easy to traverse as savanna or even
desert, and the area of governments could not be as
extended as in the Western Sudan. Still, some impressively complex governments were evolved in Ashanti
and Dahomey, Oyo and Benin, Bamun and Congo.
Our knowledge of these kingdoms is due to the fact that
some still exist today or existed until very recently, and
anthropologists have been able to reconstruct their
history. In the last fifty years, the world has come to
know the bronzes of the Yoruba peoples of Western
Nigeria or of Benin, the gold weights of Ashanti, the
masks of the Senufu or Baule.

When we measure the achievements of these societies
—and lack of them among other tribal groups—we
must do it against the background of the fact that since
1444, the only period about which we know anything
much at all, millions of Africans, often the healthiest
among them, have been taken out of Africa by the
slave trade. It is hard to overestimate the havoc—

direct and indirect—this trade caused or how it cor-
rupted area after area of Africa. The Europeans and
the Arabs, by creating and sustaining this trade, were
in part responsible for the decline of higher culture in
tropical Africa which later generations of Europeans
were to deplore.

The other great arena of African achievement was
centered on the eastern coast of Africa, starting from
present-day Kenya down to the Transvaal and extending westward into Southern Rhodesia. And here, once
again thanks to Arabic chronicles, we have written
records. The oldest we know is a record of his travels by
al-Masudi, a native of Baghdad, who in 955 described
his voyage as far as Madagascar. And in 1154, al-Idrisi
wrote for a Norman king a second-hand account of life
on the east coast of Africa, which he compiled by research into existing sources. What they described were
flourishing Iron Age cultures engaged in wide trade
across the Indian Ocean.

The Indian Ocean played a role analogous to that of
the Sahara, permitting the diffusion of technology and
the expansion of trade, so as to provide the economic
and technological base on which to build strong centralized states. Trade with Greece, Alexandria and
Rome probably can be traced at least to the first century A.D., and by the time our first chroniclers wrote,
Arab traders were installed as far south as present-day
Mozambique, as they were in South Asian and Chinese
ports. Thus it was that India was the most important
market and supplier for East Africa, a link that still
exists in altered form today. Indian beads found in
East Africa date back to the eighth century A.D. While
the Indians sold textiles in Africa, Africa exported iron
to India and ivory to China, and gold and tortoise shell
to both. And Africa even sold slaves as early as the
seventh century A.D. to Mesopotamia (for we know of
slave revolts), but slave trading was at that time not
the central focus of trade which it was to become in the

nineteenth century. China's expansion touched Africa
even before the arrival of the white men. Chinese
mariners certainly landed in East Africa in the fifteenth
century, and we have found in Africa Chinese coins and
porcelain of the twelfth century.

What kinds of cultures were these that had such far-
flung trading partners? Ethiopia is not, properly speaking, one of these cultures, but recent archaeological
findings seem to indicate a closer relationship between
Ethiopia and these cultures than we previously sus-
pected, so it is perhaps well to remind ourselves of
Ethiopia's history. Ethiopia, perhaps more than any
other part of Africa, in the eyes of the Western world
has been surrounded with legend—beginning with the
one that it was founded in 1000 B.C. by King Solomon's
son and the Queen of Sheba. Our authentic records go
back only to the first century A.D., and it was in the
fourth century that Coptic Christianity was introduced.
The arrival of Islam in the seventh century cut the
Ethiopians off from the coast and caused the kingdom's
decline. The restoration of the Solomonian line in 1270
led to a political, cultural and literary revival. It was
about this time that the legend of Prester John, that
mythical and fabulous Christian king, began to spread
in Europe. In the sixteenth century the Portuguese
arrived and Jesuit priests followed, to be expelled in
the seventeenth century. Ethiopia was not merely a
kingdom which by its cohesion survived two thousand
years. It was a culture which developed the hillside
terracing that contemporary agronomists have rediscovered as indispensable to a rational agriculture in
this part of the world.

Terracing and the art of building in dry stone—
another Ethiopian achievement—seem to be shared
with (to have been exported to?) the other cultures of
East and Central Africa. We find it, for example, in the
so-called Azanian civilization of Kenya, which is
thought to have started between 500 and 700 A.D. As

the tribal legends of many of the West Africans tell
of migrations from the east (Meroë?), so the histories
of East African tribes speak of migration from north to
south (Meroë through Ethiopia?). The Azanians seem
to come to an end about 1500. Why? The fourteenth
century seems to have been a time of invasions from
pastoral nomads, whose impact on the settled agricultural peoples seems to parallel the impact of Moroccan
conquests of Ghana and Songhay. Destructive of the
political systems, the agricultural techniques, and
scorning manual work, they left little of continuing
value in their wake. The Indian Ocean trade that sus-
tained these civilizations was coming into sharp decline
because of European expansion.

Further south, in the present-day Rhodesias and
Mozambique, was Zimbabwe culture. This included
many states built around stone forts. The Portuguese
encountered the Monomotapa, king of Benametapa,
in the sixteenth century, and his kingdom spread from
the hinterland of Mozambique through Rhodesia. But
the earliest-known kingdom may date from 500 A.D.
The Mapungubwe site in the Transvaal seems to have
been settled before 900 A.D., Great Zimbabwe itself in
the thirteenth century.

Great Zimbabwe, now the most famous ruins in
southern Africa, once the center of a controversy about
the role of the Negro in African history, is not too far
from Salisbury, present-day capital of Southern Rhodesia. The two outstanding buildings have been named
—by Europeans—the "Acropolis" and the "temple"
(or "elliptical building"). From a distance the "elliptical
building," on the plain beneath the "Acropolis," takes
on the picture of a solid fortress, with strong battle-
ments. Using local granite, the people of Zimbabwe
constructed a complex building, 300 feet long, 220 feet
broad, whose walls were 20 feet thick and 30 feet tall.
The stepped recesses and covered passages, the gate-
ways and the platforms were all hewed out elaborately,
and inside, all about, were soapstone bird-gods.

We might know more today about what was produced by the gold smelters of Zimbabwe had the British South Africa Company not given a concession to a prospector in 1895 to exploit the ruins. By the time he was stopped in 1902 the copper and gold objects were largely destroyed and melted down. Fortunately, more recently, we have discovered similar objects at Mapungubwe, unravaged by Europeans with a civilizing mission, and we can guess at what we have lost.

The various societies that were the Zimbabwe culture lasted at least a thousand years. They constructed in stone both defensive sites and dams for irrigation. They raised cattle, sowed grain, and traded across the Indian Ocean. Their chiefs enjoyed fine pottery or china, possessed gold ornaments, wore beads from India.

It was a warring culture. Or why would they have needed forts? The societies were highly stratified, with specialized craftsmen and miners, chiefs and priests. There was no system of writing, although Arabic served the coastal areas as Latin did Europe. And Swahili spread as did European vernaculars. Currencies were in use and trade was extensive. Even after the decline of the Zimbabwe kingdoms, there was no anarchy. Later missionaries were to comment on the comparative peace and security that reigned in the interior, at least in those parts less affected by the slave trade.

Yet of course this civilization did decline. These kingdoms had long been fighting off barbarian invaders. The Portuguese intruders, moreover, sacked the coastal cities and thereby sharply reduced the Indian Ocean trade, and this seems to have been a severe blow to the Zimbabwe peoples. The Portuguese with their firearms sallied into the interior, taking sides without too much knowledge (an error to be repeated by others in twentieth-century Africa?), and succeeded in undermining the whole structure. They were too weak to establish a colonial administration, only strong enough to destroy.

With the Portuguese in East Africa and in the Congo,

we enter a new era in African history. It becomes a story in which European skills and values, virtues and villainies play a major role. It is a story of how Africans reacted to their conquest by seeking to learn the secret of their weaknesses in order to reëstablish the autonomous control of their own destiny.

Before we tell this story, we should perhaps rapidly survey the kinds of social structures the Europeans did find when they came to conquer, to trade, and to preach. Every society was not Great Zimbabwe. The range was very wide. And the fact of colonial administration in each case had a somewhat different impact, depending on what was there before. Adequate categories of African tribes are difficult to establish, and for our purposes, less important than an outline of the dimensions along which tribal structures varied.

It is said that the government of tribes is based on kinship. Strictly speaking, this is seldom, perhaps never, true. It comes closest to being true among those small nomadic bands, found, say, among the Bushmen. At the other end of the continuum are those complex empires whose history we have been recounting, where the territorial (rather than ethnic) basis of government is clear. Each tribe, though, even if nomadic, does have an area it considers its own. Some Europeans challenged the veracity of this and sometimes appropriated land that was "unowned." Later, however, anthropologists demonstrated that land was rarely "unowned."

The extent of land, the number of people involved, and the cultural homogeneity of the group within one political community naturally varied. So did the organizing principle of the kinship system. Some systems were patrilineal but many, unlike societies in the Western world, were matrilineal. When more and more land was turned to the production of crops for a money market, the principle of inheritance mattered greatly.

Religious systems varied widely. Some of these systems, as we are only discovering today, attained a very

impressive complexity in the elaboration of their cosmological ideas. The complexity of the religious con-
ceptions was not necessarily related to the complexity
of the political structure. For example, one of the most
celebrated African cosmologies is that of the Dogon
(located in present-day Mali), whose society is without
commandment or police force and maintains a minimum
of social differentiation. The degree to which religious
and political functions were vested in the same man or
group of men differed, although almost everywhere the
chief had some religious role.

The splitting of religious and political functions, like
the degree of social stratification of the tribe, often
derived from patterns of conquest. As we have seen,
the African continent knew great migrations of peoples,
experienced many conquests. When the Europeans
arrived they found many situations comparable to that
of the emirates of Northern Nigeria, where a small
Fulani "aristocracy" had installed themselves as rulers
over Hausa communities. In some areas the degree of
integration was greater than in others. Sometimes the
European colonial administration would side with the
indigenous rulers and sometimes with the others.

Tribes would differ, perhaps most of all, in terms of
the role of the chief. The Asantehene or the Morho
Naba was the apex of a very complicated and extensive
hierarchy of rulers, reaching down through several tiers
to a village chief. They had courts and courtiers. At the
other extreme, there might be nothing but an ill-defined
gerontocracy, a village council with few judicial or
police powers. The chiefs who headed centralized kingdoms had men to assist them. There were wide ranges
in the functions of these men and in the way they were
recruited. Sometimes, as in medieval Europe or Japan,
the subordinate hierarchies were also hereditary.

All of these variations affected the privileges and
powers of the chief. Almost never could an African
chief be said to have absolute power. Sometimes the

constraints on his authority were so severe—when he was seldom allowed to leave his hut, or spoke to his people only through intermediaries—that it could be doubted he had any power at all. Normally decisions were the result of some consensus, though the process of consultation varied. Sometimes there were age groups to protect the interests of the "commoners," or sometimes "secret societies." In many tribes chiefs could be removed—in West Africa the word is "destooled." Later European colonial administrators sometimes destroyed the delicate balance of democratic controls. Succession was often hereditary, but even then, it might be hereditary only in the sense that the successor had to come from a certain lineage, so that there remained a wide range of choice for a new chief.

Africa before the Europeans came? It was neither anarchy nor barbarism, nor unchanged and unchanging villages. It was movement and splendor, conquests and innovations, trade and art. It was above all wide variety and much experimentation. There is no single or simple stereotype we can call "old Africa," against which we can measure how far Africa has evolved today. This is as true of Africa as of medieval Europe, where Roman gens and Scottish clan, Benedictine monk and Druid priest combined to form a varied backdrop against which the Reformation and the Renaissance, the Enlightenment and the Industrial Revolution, all evolved into a movement we have come to call modernization. Neither the multiplicity of European tribes, nor the multiplicity of African tribes, prevents us from seeing certain common features of social change which have occurred in modern times.

It is rewarding neither to denigrate nor to romanticize Africa's past. It can be rewarding to know it.

The Colonial Era

:II:

THE SOCIAL CHANGE

The expansion of Europe was part of the modernization of Europe. In the fifteenth century, the Portuguese first reached West Africa, then South and East Africa, to be followed soon thereafter by other European powers. Along one narrow strip alone, the shoreline of the Gold Coast, forts were established between the fifteenth and eighteenth centuries by Portugal, England, France, Holland, Denmark, Sweden, and Brandenburg.

At first Europeans came mainly to trade and were satisfied with outposts along the shoreline of Africa. This limited interest was reinforced in southern Africa by a geological fact. The coastal strip was very thin. As soon as one went into the interior, the land climbed rapidly above sea level and penetration became more difficult. The degree of evolution of Europe's economy also set limits on the extent of the trade. The raw materials that Europeans most sought—gold and ivory and slaves—were best provided by African intermediaries.

Along with traders came missionaries, and already in 1518 the Portuguese could celebrate in Rome the consecration of the first Negro bishop (at least since the days of early Christianity in North Africa), Henrique of the Congo, the son of the king. The missionaries came not to buy, but to sell. And so they were more inclined to push into the interior than the merchants.

Yet by and large they could not, with success, penetrate areas where they did not have the moral, material, and sometimes military support of other white men. That is why today Christianity is often strongest along the coastline, especially in West Africa.

Then, too, adventurers, soldiers, explorers came. They came to find new worlds, to track down ancient mysteries. And with them often came the flag. The merchants and missionaries also demanded the flag, for their safety, to reinforce their own positions. Still, at the beginning of the nineteenth century, very few parts of Africa were under European rule. The Portuguese colonies—Angola, Mozambique, Guinea, São Tomé e Principe—were already established. The Cape Colony, at the southern tip of Africa, had passed from Dutch to English rule in 1795. Senegal had become a French colony in the eighteenth century, and the Gambia and Sierra Leone became British colonies in the latter half of the eighteenth century. In each case, the area of the colony was much less extensive then than the area with the corresponding name today. The largest portion of the African continent was still self-governing. By 1880 the situation was not too different; only a few other coastal strips, such as the Gaboon, Lagos, the Gold Coast, and Algeria, had become colonial states. Suddenly, for reasons internal to Europe, there started a race to colonize all of Africa. This race was assigned legitimacy by the Congress of Berlin (1884–85), which laid out the ground rules whereby European powers would allow each other to divide up the African pie. By 1900 there was scarcely a corner of Africa that had escaped European rule. Liberia and Ethiopia were the two significant exceptions, and even Ethiopia had suffered an Italian protectorate from 1889–96.

The motivations that led individual Europeans to come to Africa, as settlers, as traders, as teachers, varied widely. There was the lure of adventure, the search for personal freedom, the sense of mission. There was greed

and vanity and lust for power. The motives that led
European powers to sanction expansion and to establish permanent colonial rule also varied. There was the
search for markets and resources, the need for prestige
and power, the sense of historic mission (as with some
individuals). Whatever it was that brought about
colonial rule, it is certain that once a colonial administration was established, something very important
happened. For now all the things that men and groups
did in Africa, they did within the context of the *colonial
situation.*

By the term *colonial situation* we simply mean that
someone imposes in a given area a new institution, the
colonial administration, governed by outsiders who
establish new rules which they enforce with a reasonable degree of success. It means that all those who act
in the colony must take some account of these rules,
and that indeed an increasing amount of each individual's action is oriented to this set of rules rather
than to any other set, for example, the tribal set, to
which he formerly paid full heed. The reason for this
shift in orientation is very simple. Colonial administration, as opposed to the mere presence of European
traders or missionaries, meant precisely that ultimate
power lay with this new government, and that this
government tried systematically to inculcate in its
subjects a feeling that this new power was legitimate.
To a certain extent, this attempt to legitimate colonial
rule in Africa was temporarily successful, partly because
of the great physical power of the Europeans, partly
because the social changes that colonial rule introduced
produced changes in the attitudes of Africans, particularly the new elites, toward the colonial government.

What were these changes? There were many economic changes, first of all. In the late nineteenth and
early twentieth centuries, the merchants of Liverpool
and Bordeaux and Hamburg expanded their operations,
and networks of trading houses grew up. The day of the

great export-import house in Africa was beginning.
Importing Manchester cloth, household wares, bicycles
and other appurtenances of Western civilization, these
companies became the major, often the only, channels
for the export of raw materials. Nor were they satisfied,
as were their forebears, with simply acquiring those
precious goods that were readily available. They sought
to stimulate their production. Southern Africa had the
most profitable mineral deposits—gold and diamonds
in the Transvaal, copper in Northern Rhodesia, diamonds and tin in the Congo—but there was mining in
West Africa as well.*

Great trading networks, mines, *and* administrations
needed men, African men, to do the work, at least all
but the higher managerial tasks. They needed men,
furthermore, who had some of the skills necessary to
do the work, and some of the values that would make
them willing to do it. And it was difficult at first to find
large numbers of such men, particularly for work in the
mines or the ports or on engineering projects.

While some African cultures had used sophisticated
productive techniques and some were characterized by
a market economy, the majority of the population
everywhere was engaged in a subsistence economy.
Even where African societies were complex kingdoms,
the village remained the traditional center of African
life. The frame of custom was strong. Money was relatively unimportant (sometimes nonexistent), as the internal economy of the village was communal. In the
natural course of events, the villager would not leave
his village. The new colonial economy, however, required manpower, and if the needs were to be met, the
villagers had to be induced to leave their villages and
come to town and mine compound to work. The towns
were created because towns were, in Africa as through-

* In the period since World War II, vast new resources have
been uncovered, such as oil in the Sahara, iron in Mauritania,
and iron in Liberia.

out the world, efficient centers of administration, production and trade, and communications. A modern economy required urban centers, and these centers taught men urban, that is modern, values.

One way to induce men to leave villages was to force them to do so. Slave trading by and large came to an end in the middle of the nineteenth century, partly as a result of humanitarian pressures in the Western world, partly because slavery was no longer economic in the advanced technologies of the nineteenth century. Outright slavery was not used within Africa. But forced labor was.* The usual method was for the colonial administration to give chiefs quotas to fill. Sometimes the *corvées* were used on public projects, and sometimes on the private enterprises of Europeans. As the years went by, and Africans for various reasons were more willing to enter the money economy, the recruitment methods tended more toward persuasion. Indeed, in more recent years, elaborate recruiting organizations have been established to advertise the virtues of labor migration.

There were other ways of indirectly forcing men to migrate to the towns. The appropriation of land by European farmers, which occurred throughout settler Africa (French North Africa, Kenya, Southern Rhodesia, the Union of South Africa), led in time, sometimes immediately, to land squeezes among Africans, especially since Africans had been forced back onto less productive lands. And a classic remedy for a land squeeze, as anyone acquainted with recent European history must remember, is emigration. The appropriation of land by European settlers occurred, however, only where the climate was sufficiently moderate, the land sufficiently fertile to make it worth the while of white farmers. West and Equatorial Africa, for example, had very few settlers, and in many areas there was

* It still is used in Portuguese Africa, in 1961, and in a variant form (as punishment for violation of pass laws) in the Republic of South Africa.

express legislation which forbade the alienation of land
to Europeans.

There was another weapon of indirect pressure available to the colonia authorities, that of the head tax.
The head tax, in one form or another, was introduced
throughout Africa, and imposed often over serious
African objection. In a village which lived on its own
produce and used no currency, even the smallest tax
raised a demand which could not be met within the
village. Either the whole village would have to engage
itself somehow in the money economy, or as happened
more often because it was easier, the village had to ask
some of its younger men to sally forth into the towns
to earn the money that would enable the village to pay
the head tax for all its citizens. Thus, the sentiment of
community solidarity of the village, under the pressure
of the colonial situation, led to the exporting of its men
into a new and often alien world, a process which in its
turn would usually lead to a breakdown of this very
sentiment of community solidarity.

The colonial administration did not forever have to
force men to migrate from the villages. After a while,
the town itself lured them. They began to want the
things the city has offered since it first was invented:
the relative freedom from the pressures of one's neighbors, the opportunities for social advancement, the
possibility of participation in a wider range of social
activities. And they began to want the things that
money could buy: material comforts, a longer and
healthier life, contacts with a wider world.

These new values were the result, at least in part, of
three major elements of colonial rule. For reasons internal to itself, and deriving from its own needs, colonial
administration brought with it order, modern education, and improved transport and communications.
Each of these was to play a major role in changing the
perspectives of the African.

Order, of course, existed before the European came,

sometimes within very large areas. Often the first result
of European penetration was the breakdown of well-
established order. Still, colonial order was established
more or less in most parts of Africa by 1900, although
parts of Mauritania were officially "pacified" only as
late as 1934. After 1945, of course, the new disorder of
nationalist ferment was to begin throughout the continent.

Colonial order was new in that the colonial power
treated as one unit what had previously not been one,
an area usually a good deal larger than that of a particular tribe. Indeed, as has been observed before, colonial
boundaries quite often ran through the boundaries of
given tribes. European colonial order was also new in
that it introduced new cultural perspectives to the
African, which meant acquaintance with new ideas,
involvement in new groups, the possibility of new
movement.

Colonial order meant, first of all, that in this new
political unit larger than the tribe there was some possibility of safe movement. In some areas this was true for
the first time; in others this new freedom of movement
restored and reinforced a reality which had existed before. The fact of colonial order had a very important
impact on the psychology of the villager and hence on
the structure of control in the African village. The dis-
senter, the misfit, the rebel could now defy the chief
simply by moving out from under his control. He could
"escape" to the city. Needless to say, this often made
it possible to attract to town life precisely those people
with the initiative and imagination to break with tradition, to try new ways, to seek a better fortune outside
the path laid out for them. The best—and the worst—
came to the city, because there was a city to come to.

Order not only affected the chance of the deviant to
live his life in a context that suited him better; it also
affected the lives of whole classes of people in tribal
societies. For example, the tribal warrior—in many

tribes warriors were a separate social group, in some a full-time occupation—became bereft of any useful function in his group. He could enlist in the army of the colonial government. But if he did, he was fatally introduced to modern skills and values. In many African countries where men enlisted, the returned ex-serviceman became not only a major agent of social change in the village but, except when constantly and carefully cultivated by the local administration, an early exponent of nationalist ideas.

In some tribes, warfare was linked to a boy's initiation into manhood and his assumption of full responsibility in tribal life. Where the colonial administration closed off this channel of testing virility and valor, tribal societies had to invent alternatives. One possibility was to consider a stint in a mine equivalent to achievements as a warrior. Some might argue that, especially in the early days of colonial rule, this experience demonstrated far more than earlier tests one's fitness to survive.

Order within the colony had another consequence. It became possible for traders to move about or to resume movement within the colony, where before warring tribes forbade entry. Quite often in West as in East Africa, the trading communities were Moslem; they spread both the relatively modern values that their commercial activities encouraged as well as Islam, which, insofar as it was a world religious community, involved its adherents in currents and ideas broader and more modern than those of many African tribal societies. Before the colonial era there were areas where the expansion of Islam had been stopped by the force of a strong animist kingdom; colonial rule allowed Moslem traders (and preachers, for each Moslem is in a limited sense called upon to be a preacher of his religion) to enter for the first time.

Just as maintaining order was in the self-interest of the colonial power, so too was the extension of modern

educational facilities to Africa; it was not a gratuitous
gift of benevolent Europe. A modern economy, however
limited in scope, needs men to run it, to work its mines,
to staff its offices, to drive its vehicles. It needs not any
men, but *trained* men. The colonial government needed
such men; so did the private trading companies; so did
the missions, the schools, and the hospitals. Schools for
children are the most economical and effective way of
producing them. Therefore schools were started everywhere. The Catholic and Protestant missionaries played
an important role in the establishment of these schools,
financing and staffing a larger percentage of them in
African countries than in European countries. But the
colonial governments everywhere established schools as
well. In the Moslem areas (North Africa, Northeast
Africa, large parts of the interior of West Africa), the
colonial authorities often kept the missions out for fear
of offending Moslem sensibilities.

Of course, educational facilities were not established
exclusively for functional reasons. Ordinarily, there was
no simple calculation made of how many people were
needed to keep the economy going—although this happened more often than one would think—and therefore
how many schools should be opened. There were many
Europeans who "believed" in education. Some Christian
missionaries saw it as a fundamental aspect of the process of conversion. Some colonial administrators felt they
had a "civilizing mission." A passion was aroused for
education for its own sake, which sometimes led to the
creation of more educated Westernized men than were
needed for the pace of economic development; and this
caused strains in the structures of various colonies that
contributed to the emergence of nationalist movements.

Colonial government also required the improvement
and expansion of facilities for transportation and communication within the colony in order to assure efficient
administration, the maintenance of order, and the maxi-
mization of economic growth and profit. Thus railroad

lines were built, roads and airports constructed, tele-
graph wires installed. Economic rationality was, to be
sure, conceived of only within the framework of a
single colony, or at best within the framework of the
colonies of a single colonial power. Thus we have the
resulting mad pattern of today: two roads stopping five
miles from each other with no connection because of a
boundary line, as between the Congo and Uganda; two
railroad lines, parallel to each other and not too distant,
running from port to inland on different gauges with
no link between them because each was in the territory
of a different colonial power, as in Nigeria and Dahomey, or Guinea and Sierra Leone.

The pattern of transport and communications, looked
at from an overall African viewpoint, was quixotic.
Much later the independent states of Africa would
turn their attention to overcoming this obstacle to their
closer relations. Furthermore, economic development,
even within a single colony, principally served to link
a few people in a few centers to the outside world. It
did not create an internally integrated economy.
Nevertheless, economic improvements were important
for their political consequences, for the ways in which
they permitted men and ideas to circulate more rapidly.

The railroad brought with it, as it did on the American frontier, new economic bustle, new industries, new
horizons. Improved facilities did not merely make possible more circulation but contained a hidden multiplier
—they made possible more turnover. African villagers
could come and go; they could return to their villages
to be replaced by other villagers in the towns. Ever
larger numbers of villagers, therefore, were exposed to
urban life, even if for a short time only, and permanent
residents of the towns could visit their natal villages
more often. Thus, modernization spread, moving too
fast to be encompassed by the slow pace of colonial
economic and political development; and once again,
the strains produced would help to account for the

sudden outburst of nationalist sentiment that was to come.

The town was not merely the incubator of new values and ideas; it was also a center for the spread of these values and ideas to the villages. But the village bred its own seed of rebellion and modernism as well. The institution of cash crops was as important in the process of social change as mining. Every territory, if it was lucky, had a cash crop, but usually only one. There was wine in Algeria and cotton in the Sudan and Uganda, cocoa in the Gold Coast (Ghana) and coffee in the Ivory Coast, sisal in Tanganyika and tobacco in Southern Rhodesia. Cash crops brought money to the villages. They gave a new importance to the method of inheritance. They also brought problems of land ownership and land alienation; in some areas Europeans virtually appropriated the land.

Cash crops were sometimes introduced by Europeans on plantations, sometimes grown by African planters who were encouraged by colonial governments. Plantations were the common pattern in settler Africa, where active discouragement of African farmers in favor of Europeans sometimes occurred, as in the case of coffee in Kenya. But often in nonsettler Africa, the government would take steps directly to encourage and assist the emergence of a small-holding cash-crop peasantry—as, for example, the Gezira Scheme in the Anglo-Eyptian Sudan and the Office du Niger in French West Africa. Simply preventing alienation of land to Europeans would also serve this end—as for example, in the Gold Coast or the Western Region of Nigeria. Sometimes, as in the Ivory Coast, the African peasants would find themselves in competition with a small group of European planters, the latter having the advantages of forced labor and (by statute) better prices. Such unequal competition was to breed a strong reaction.

The introduction of a cash crop could not help but

change the traditional social structure somewhat. Often
it required different work patterns. Usually it meant
that there began to grow up a distinction between land
on which food was grown, which remained communal
land, and land on which cash crops were grown, which
tended to shift to a pattern of individual ownership.
Matriarchal systems particularly were undermined by
cash crops. Insofar as all land was part of a subsistence
economy, there was relatively little difference between
one plot and another. The young man who, having
worked on his father's land, then moves to inherit the
land of his mother's brother, which is roughly equivalent, accepts this tradition as just. But if, in a cash-crop
economy, the new plot is much poorer or perhaps not
even producing the cash crop, he is going to feel ag-
grieved. And unless the system is changed, he will be
reluctant to work hard on his father's plot, which not he,
but his cousin, will inherit.

Even where the traditional economy was left intact,
however, the rural area was to know change. Colonial
administration reached out everywhere and, in order
to stabilize its existence, created some organs of local
government. The European colonial power might try
to establish a rational bureaucratic hierarchy with all
officials operating on a state payroll and within a single
judicial framework. Efforts in this direction were called
direct administration and were often associated with
French rule. In fact, of course, complete direct administration never existed. It was too expensive, particularly
since it was difficult to find adequate numbers of indigenous personnel who had the necessary skills or to
train men rapidly. It would have meant the importation
of large numbers of Europeans who were both costly
and unavailable. Furthermore, it would have required
a very rapid and radical alteration of patterns of
government at the village level. The colonial administration was not prepared to deal with such a revolution.

What then of the opposite possibility, "indirect rule,"

leaving in place the traditional system and often the traditional ruler, and operating as much as possible through that system? This style of government has been associated with British colonial rule, and the policies of Lord Lugard in Northern Nigeria and Sir Donald Cameron in Tanganyika. And indeed it has been wide-spread in British Africa: Zanzibar, the High Commission Territories, Buganda in Uganda, Barotseland in Northern Rhodesia, the Northern Territories of the Gold Coast, the Protectorates of Sierra Leone and the Gambia. Although indirect rule is often thought of as a British monopoly, French policy in Morocco, Belgian policy in Ruanda-Urundi show close parallels.

Indirect rule never meant the complete preservation of traditional authority. It could not, or the entire element of colonial rule would have been eliminated from it. Colonial rule, however circumscribed in its definition, required some limitation on the judicial and political authority of the traditional ruler. Once it became apparent that the chief's authority was no longer ultimate, and that the chief was subject in some areas to the authority of the district administrative officer, the power of the chief was thereby undermined. And the sharp line between direct and indirect rule was thereby blurred. In fact the line was seldom sharp in Africa; all the colonial powers evolved a pragmatic policy which involved, in one way or another, working with or through chiefs but always within the framework of overall colonial rules and values. It meant that wher-ever and to whatever degree chiefs retained power they did so at the grace of the colonial power.

One important cause of the decline of chieftaincy as an institution was the great ease with which colonial authorities, when they felt it necessary, would remove the incumbent and replace him with another. Some-times this would be the outcome of the process of over-coming African resistance ("pacification")—death, exile, or retirement for the defeated chief. Sometimes the re-

moval of a chief would be merely an error. An African
tribe would occasionally put forward a false chief as a
negotiator to safeguard the real one. Whether done
deliberately or in error, this kind of replacement at the
beginning of the colonial era created in many areas the
phenomenon of two chiefs, one having the recognition
and support of the colonial authority, one the legitimation of tradition still recognized by the villagers.

But this initial replacement was perhaps less important than the continuing strain on the chief under
colonial rule. For whether administration was direct or
indirect, colonial rule tended to devolve upon the chief
more and more administrative tasks for the colonial
authority. The chief was variously expected to enforce
colonial law, impress labor, collect taxes. These were
not merely administrative tasks; they were unpopular
ones. The chief found his role beginning to shift from
that of spokesman for his people to that of agent of the
colonial administration vis-à-vis his people. The consequence was an increasing frequency of replacement of
the chief, either by the colonial authority or, if tradition
permitted it, by the African villagers. Occasionally the
pace of replacement became so rapid as to lead to the
complete breakdown of traditional authority.

Even when such drastic events did not occur, the
very process of out-migration to the towns and in-
migration of the traders (or of rural laborers in cash-
crop areas) meant a steady pressure toward the
"territorialization" of the chief's authority—at which
point, a demand would grow up for its "democratiza-
tion," that is, its replacement by an elected village
council. Another steady pressure against the traditional
authority of the chief was the spread of Christianity,
where it did spread. For the Christian villager would
refuse to engage in the traditional religious ceremonies
of the village, and by extension, would begin to challenge the whole authority of the ruler.

As we have seen, the economic changes, the spread of

education, the immigration to the towns, all led to the growth of a new elite, one not necessarily recruited from among those who had status and authority in the traditional social system. Quite often the opposite was true. This new elite, whether in the town or back in the village, simply was not willing to give the same deference or recognition of authority to the chief as previously. The younger generation had found new sources of reward, new identifications with European and/or modern values, new evaluations of their own achievements.

It was the emergence of this new elite that was the single most important consequence of the social change brought about by colonial rule. Traditional authority, weakened by the assaults of colonial rule (even, ironically, when the latter tried to maintain it, as in indirect rule), was further threatened by the refusal of this new elite to subordinate itself to a system in which it had no place and whose values seemed to it outmoded. This new elite began to react—not merely against traditional rulers, but against the colonial rulers as well.

:III:

THE REACTION

The men of the new elite bred by the colonial administration were "Westernized," that is, they began to learn and share the values of Western civilization, at least in part. Furthermore, they began to *want to be* Westernized. They began to model themselves on the Europeans with whom they came in contact—in religion, in comportment, in style of life. And European administrators, particularly in the nonsettler territories at the beginning of the colonial era, actively encouraged them in this path. It was flattering and useful for colonial governments to have an intermediate social grouping that copied European social patterns.

But once again, social change in Africa outstripped European expectations. As the new African elite studied European history in the African schools—for there was no African history considered worthy of study—and as they studied in Europe, they became more and more aware of a great egalitarian movement occurring within European society itself. The rise of individualist philosophy in the West, of the doctrine of the inherent rights of all human beings to liberty and equality became a familiar story to them—the Reformation and the Renaissance, the Enlightenment, the French Revolution, the nineteenth-century achievement throughout Europe of wider suffrage, increasing guarantees against arbitrary government, and the slow emergence of labor and socialist movements designed to extend the gains of bourgeois democracy by creating economic and social conditions that would allow the lower classes to profit fully from the advantages of a free society.

Alongside this current of ideas and institutional change was another development which for a long time ran parallel to it. The end of the Middle Ages was marked by the creation of a new political structure, the nation-state. At first focused around an absolute monarch, the nation-state came increasingly to be built around the concept of a sovereign people. The French and American Revolutions crystallized this convergence of the forces of nationalism and the forces of liberalism. The Napoleonic empire encouraged the spread of these forces, and the various revolutions of 1848 were the culmination of their coalescence. Even after this period, in southern and eastern Europe, liberalism and nationalism went hand in hand. Just as men demanded equal rights as individuals and as classes of individuals, so did they demand equal rights as nations. The right to create and maintain nationhood came to be associated with the fight for freedom, a point of view illustrated by a statement made by Hobhouse in 1911: "National and personal freedom are growths of the same root."

In some ways the Russian revolution was a culmination of these nineteenth-century movements. It was a triumph of European egalitarian ideology. But it also meant the liberation of Russia from the cultural and intellectual hegemony of Western Europe. Russia became an equal, independent participant in the formulation of Western ideology. In freeing itself from the domination of the West, Russia opened the way for colonial intellectuals to break with the West too without rejecting it altogether. It opened the way not only in intellectual terms but in terms of creating a new world power situation which facilitated the long-range process of decolonization.

Before the First World War, even to a large extent before the Second World War, Africa was remote from these events. African problems were not generally analyzed by Europeans in terms of these egalitarian principles. Nor were most Africans specifically aware of these European developments and their implications for Africa. There was one important link, though—the small group of intellectuals that had come into existence in the colonies, particularly those who had been to European universities or others who had traveled in Europe (as, for example, soldiers during the wars). These men had acquired European values; indeed egalitarian principles had been taught to them specifically, to some extent in colonial schools, more emphatically in metropolitan universities.

In addition to lessons on the merits of equality these men also had received training in various occupations and professions leading them to expect advancement in careers which they were not in fact allowed to have. Men trained as engineers could find no employment because it would not do to have an African engineer supervise a white foreman. As Chief Awolowo of Nigeria said as late as 1946: "Only a few parents so far have had the courage to send their sons abroad to study engineering. African engineers did not succeed in getting jobs under the Government or Native Administrations." Men trained as lawyers, especially in the settler territories, knew that they would never become judges. A clerk never, or very rarely, could rise to be head of a government department. And on a simpler level, sergeants could never become lieutenants. At whatever level of skill, Africans had to curb their ambitions because in the colonial situation governments were reluctant, often formally opposed, to making any exceptions in a structure where European ruled African.

And in that intermediate plane where European and African held the same job, the pay scales were widely different, at least until the rise of the nationalist movements after World War II.

Nor was this all. The colonial political structure was an autocracy with the governor at its head, where the citizen had no political rights or very few. It is true that, as time went on, a few municipal or legislative councils were established, in which members were elected (often on a property suffrage); however, they were usually in a minority or did not have significant powers vis-à-vis the administrators. In settler territories, lack of even such minor political devolution to Africans was aggravated by the turning over of power, exclusively or disproportionately, to white settlers.

Thus, the African intellectuals—and more generally, urbanized Africans—were limited in their careers and denied access to political power. Yet the people who demanded the vote and job advancement were precisely those who had broken with the traditional elite and had acquired egalitarian values. They defined this limitation and denial as a frustration, an unjust frustration. What is more, this definition was one which most Europeans, to be consistent with their own values, had to accept as valid.

Africans, then, came to demand equality, and equality not only in the political arena but in all aspects of life: economic equality, educational equality, religious equality, cultural equality. The same theme would arise in many different guises, sometimes fitfully, not always coördinated with demands in other fields, not always accorded acceptance in European circles—even those of the intellectual left. The core of the demand, however, was a political one—equal participation in political decisions that affect all within the community. The question of course arose: which community? Some defined the community as the imperial network; others as the colony.

Demands for political equality in the imperial network meant giving an African exactly the same rights as a European *living in Europe*—voting, access to education and career, equality of pay and living standards. This was the logical consequence of a policy of political assimilation and was particularly favored in French Africa. Early demands of Algerian, Senegalese, Malagasy intellectuals were often phrased in terms of the ultimate objective of becoming part of France, which was moreover officially proclaimed the object of French colonization by many theorists of the empire. Full citizenship was a prime demand. Education, social and economic development were advocated to make the granting of full citizenship possible and meaningful. Assimilation—that is, becoming part of France—meant the renunciation of African culture and adoption of the patterns and ways of life of the metropolitan community.

Ultimately, however, assimilation as a road to political equality came to be rejected in Africa, not because it did not solve the problem theoretically, but because it was so nearly impossible to implement, at least within any reasonable span of time. It was tempting to the intellectuals since they could presumably benefit from it immediately if they had the support of the "liberal" administrators. But the concept that all Africans *as individuals* would be admitted to equal rights in the imperial system was translated very quickly into a formula best summarized by Cecil Rhodes's famous slogan, "Equal rights for all civilized men." Formulated this way, it made admission to political equality a privilege for Africans, contingent on their passing certain tests administered by Europeans, who could thereby control not only admission to these rights but the overall rate of admission. In practice very few were admitted. Africans came to consider the path of assimilation a lure. Even had perfect good will and fairness existed on all sides, it was inevitable that this process

be slow, as its accomplishment demanded the complete
abandonment of traditional cultures by African peasant
masses, whose education and contact with the modern
economic world ranged from nonexistent to minor.
Moreover, as time went on, African intellectuals began
to ask, with some justice, why it should automatically
be assumed that it is an unadulterated virtue to accept
Western values. We shall examine this contention in
detail later on, when we discuss cultural revival.

And so, assimilation having failed, perhaps because
(as some say of Christianity) it had never been tried,
these intellectuals turned to where others had started,
the alternate path to political equality: political separation, that is, national independence. Here the demand
was not that individual African be placed alongside
individual European in equal status, but that Africans
as a group be equal to Europeans as a group, both being
organized into sovereign nations.

The classic example of this reversal in attitude is the
personal political path of Ferhat Abbas. In 1936,
Ferhat Abbas, then advocating assimilation, said: "If
I had discovered 'the Algerian nation,' I should have
become a nationalist, and should not have blushed for
it. . . . I did not find it. I consulted history, the living
and the dead. . . . You cannot build on air. We have
discarded once and for all the nonsense and the chi-
meras definitely to align our future with that of the
French work in our country. Six million Moslems live
on this soil which has been French for a hundred years;
they live in hovels, go barefoot, without clothing and
often without bread. Out of this hungry mass we shall
make a modern society . . . elevate them to human
dignity so that they may be worthy of the name of
Frenchmen." In 1958 Ferhat Abbas became Premier of
the Provisional Government of the Algerian Republic,
advocating independence for Algeria.

Obviously, even when national independence was the
ultimate goal, it usually was not made the immediate

demand at first. What was called for was the steady
creation of more organs of representative government
with more real powers, the transfer of power from
colonial authority, embodied in the governor, to African
people. The series of demands, each leading to the next,
was like the series that Western Europe witnessed internally with respect to the transfer of authority from
the king to a parliament elected by universal suffrage.

There were many colonies where these demands were
not considered legitimate, either because the colonial
ideology stressed assimilation (French, Portuguese) or
because settler control led to the development of an
antidemocratic ideology (white supremacy in the
Union of South Africa). Sometimes, even when nationalism was proscribed as an ideology by the colonial
adminstration, alternate political outlets were provided
because the ideology of assimilation was to some extent
taken seriously (French North Africa, Senegal). But
there were some cases where no political outlets, or
almost none, were permitted to any group of Africans,
particularly before the end of the Second World War.
This was true, for example, of the Belgian Congo,
French Equatorial Africa, Angola and Mozambique.
This was also true, in varying degrees, of different parts
of English-speaking southern Africa from the Union of
South Africa to Kenya. It is no accident that these
areas saw the greatest flourishing of nativistic, revival-
istic and syncretistic movements, quite often clothed in
religious garb (Kitiwala, Kimbanguism, Alice cult,
Mau Mau). Where no political outlets for grievances
were permitted, at least to the small elite, they or their
followers often turned to pseudotraditional patterns
which were, on the one hand, more familiar and easy to
handle, and on the other hand, could appeal to a legitimation which even colonial rulers accepted to some
extent: religious freedom. In short, political protest did
not always or necessarily take a political form. To see
the nationalist movements in their proper perspective,

it is important to see the rise of political associations in the towns and then in the rural areas as just one element in the steady growth of whole networks of voluntary associations based on the desires and needs of Africans to group together to resolve mutual problems or advance mutual aims within the emerging modern societies of which they were now a part.

The first problem faced by the new urban dweller was not that of achieving equality. It was that of providing some kind of system of social security for himself in this new money-oriented world. It was that of filling the void created when he was cut off from his traditional social ways which had resulted in feelings of uncertainty and loneliness. The urban African was uprooted and hence needed new assurances of economic well-being, new groups of which he could be a part and within which he could re-establish the moral limits of his action. This has been the need and the response of rural migrants to the towns everywhere in the world.

What the family and tribe could not provide because they were disrupted, what the colonial government could not provide because it had not the material means and personnel, nor the confidence of its subjects, urban Africans provided for themselves by creating new organizations. The first to organize were usually the educated. Throughout the continent one of the commonest forms of organization was the alumni association, formed by secondary schools, technical schools, sometimes—if nothing else existed—upper primary schools. It was a natural grouping, one to which colonial authorities could object only with difficulty, one which appealed to the immediate interests of the group who were most apt to have the skills necessary to organize an association. Quite often these associations were disguised trade unions where trade unionism was still forbidden. They grouped together civil servants or schoolteachers or professionals who had common frustrations and common grievances against the colonial

administration. As time went by, many of these groups
would transform themselves into proper trade unions or
become the base for a political party. These groups were
an important means of political action before it was
legal as well as a valuable training ground for later
nationalist activity.

Alumni associations were not the only form such
groupings of the educated took. Westernized Africans
formed social clubs, dancing classes, literary discussion
circles. They formed sports associations in order to play
the European games they had learned in schools and to
associate with each other. Sometimes a group would be
formed on an ethnic basis and would set itself the
explicit task of raising the educational and social level
of its home village; thus the association, as an instru-
ment of modernization, would be brought to the rural
areas, establishing an acceptable role for the educated
in traditional society, from the point of view of both the
educated and the traditionalists.

The educated were not the only ones to form groups,
though they were usually the first. The uneducated
urban dweller—the market woman, the small artisan,
the house servant—rapidly acquired the sophistication
to realize how valuable a technique this was. Friendly
and mutual-benefit societies sprang up everywhere.
Religious groups, ethnic associations, football clubs—
football, or rather soccer, rapidly became the "mass"
sport in African towns—also arose. One key element of
almost all these organizations was that they provided
cash payments to tide the individual over the major
critical turning points of life: birth of a child, marriage,
and most important of all, burial. But this function of
the groups was not merely a financial matter. It was
the means by which the group created an emotional
haven, a new "family" that could support the individual morally, help him to adjust to urban life, teach him
the techniques needed to get along.

The voluntary associations clearly were performing

very important functions, and even the colonial administration saw the virtue of some kinds of associations.
Indeed, often the administration took the lead in establishing groups in Africa on the model of organizations in European countries—youth groups, athletic
teams, and after the Second World War, even trade
unions. But from the point of view of the colonial
administration, these associations were useful only to
the extent that they served as auxiliaries to the administration. They were useful, that is, if they trained
Africans in ways of living that would enable the colony
to function better as an administrative or economic
unit. They were dangerous if they became a framework
within which social protest and political agitation could
ferment and become active.

But the very existence of voluntary associations created channels of information other than that of the
colonial government; for example, there were links with
international voluntary groups. Also, the associations
trained people in the skills of organization and of
speaking, so necessary in political life. They brought
together elements of the population who were otherwise
divided. They began, bit by bit, to escape the confines
within which the colonial government wished to keep
them and became "politicized."

One way this happened was through the creation of
autonomous, African counterparts to Western-style
groups, such as the *African* scouts, as opposed to the
Boy Scouts of given countries, and African trade unions,
which broke their links with European groups of which
they had formerly been a part. The movement for
autonomy grew even among Christian churches, where
separatist groups with African hierarchies sometimes
were created. Another way in which autonomy was
encouraged was not through the creation of Africanized
counterparts to European groups but through the establishment of new types of groups, African not only
in personnel and name but often in tradition and cul-

tural values as well. The various kinds of groups, both African and Westernized, appealed to different parts of the population, channeling different grievances. Their coördination into a single movement which gave coherent voice to their collective grievances, stressing the common underlying theme of equality, was to await the emergence of political leadership.

The earliest openly political organizations were usually offshoots of some of these early associations of the educated. They expressed limited demands for greater rights and a measure of self-rule, at least on the municipal level. One of the earliest of such movements was the African National Congress of the Union of South Africa. In North Africa, there was the Destour in Tunisia, to be followed in the 1920's by the Neo-Destour. At the same time, Messali Hadj founded the Etoile Nord-Africain among Algerians in Paris. In West Africa at the end of the First World War, there arose the National Congress of British West Africa, while in Kenya, in the 1920's, was founded the Kikuyu Central Association. In the 1930's, a Socialist federation (branch of the French SFIO), founded in Senegal, served the same purpose, and in Morocco, the Comité d'Action Marocaine was founded. It was, however, not until after World War II that similar groups were started in most other territories.

These early protonationalist groups varied in effectiveness and popular appeal. They did give voice to grievances. They did assert the right to organize and to make demands on the colonial government, thus paving the way for their successors. But by and large, they were treated lightly by the colonial government, which usually claimed that they represented no one but themselves—a small urban, highly educated minority. And in terms of the ability of these movements to mobilize mass support, there was some truth in this assertion. But the grievances of the colonial era were real. The inequalities not only existed; they were built into the system, and ideologies to justify their maintenance were propagated. Furthermore, the very processes of the colonial system, the expansion of the economy which was at its base, continued to breed, at an ever-expanding rate, the frustrated individuals who would one day revolt.

The Second World War was greatly to accelerate political organization in African societies. For one thing, many Africans served in armies in Asia, Europe, and parts of Africa other than their home territory. And European and American (including American Negro) soldiers served in North, Northeast and West Africa. The increased contact of Africa with the world stirred up new aspirations. Nigerians came into contact in India with Indian nationalists. Gold Coasters or Senegalese or Tunisians saw behavior on the part of European soldiers which they had never encountered before among European settlers or administrators, such as Europeans engaged in manual labor. The defeat and occupation of many of the colonial powers at home made a strong impression. Whatever it was, large numbers of Africans had new perspectives on the possibilities of action. Furthermore, army service and the intensified economic activity which wartime brought to Africa led to an increased training of mechanics, artisans, drivers, nurses, teachers, and others, who then formed a sizable "lower middle class" in each colony. It was this new group who, in the postwar years, would give vent to new grievances—those of colonial frustration generally, combined oftentimes with the particular complaints of ex-servicemen who had not received their due.

Meanwhile, social change in Africa was not occurring in a vacuum. The Second World War resulted in basic shifts in the world power situation. The United States and the Soviet Union became the leaders of two vast power blocs, engaged in a cold war which forced them to seek support in the non-European areas of the world. In Asia, the Japanese conquest of Southeast Asia meant

an ouster of European colonial powers which could not
be undone in the postwar era. England, under a Labor
government, showed the way by gracefully withdrawing
from India, Pakistan, Ceylon and Burma. The Netherlands left Indonesia under some pressure, and the
French left Indochina only very reluctantly and very
late. Nevertheless, they all left and the impact of Asian
independence on African developments was not small.
In Ghana the Convention People's Party adopted the
(Indian) Congress cap as their symbol. Ben Bella, one
of the leaders who started the Algerian revolution in
1954, received his military training (and political education?) as a sergeant in the French Army in Indochina.
Many African nationalist leaders throughout East,
Central and South Africa proclaimed themselves
disciples of Gandhi's technique of nonviolent resistance.

Given the changes in the internal structure of African
colonies and the international context, the majority of
African colonial territories, in the fifteen years following
the end of the war, saw the emergence of mass nationalist movements. These movements either transformed
or replaced the protonationalist groupings that had
existed. These movements, sometimes led by younger
intellectuals who had broken with their elders because
the pace of advance was too slow, made use of the
expanded "lower middle class" as the cadres of organization, thus moving out of the confines of an educated
urban elite to organize and educate urban masses in
the slums and peasants in the bush or wadi. Sometimes
the break of mass nationalist movements with urban
educated groups who had previously been the leaders
of protest movements was accompanied by real anger
against these groups for the privileged position that
they had enjoyed under the colonial regime. In West
Africa there was particular resentment against such
groups as the professional men in the Gold Coast
(Ghana), the Creoles in Sierra Leone, the Senegalese
throughout French West Africa. The half-castes and

the West Indians often suffered under such suspicion.
The attitude of Africans toward Coloureds in the
Union of South Africa was somewhat similar.

Organizing nationalist movements in African territories was not easy, for a nationalist movement is essentially a revolutionary movement. It aims not merely to
change the people in power or some of the policies of
government, but also to change the system fundamentally; in this case, it aimed to overthrow the colonial
government. Revolutionary movements can expect to
meet resistance from the powers-that-be. And African
nationalist movements did meet such resistance from
the colonial governments. In some cases, the changing
world situation put outside pressure on the colonial
powers to cede their positions, or created situations
within the metropolitan country which altered the resolve to stay. But, on the other hand, European settlers
or interest groups often could put moral and political
pressure on the colonial government, or the retention
of a colony became bound up with certain prestige or
economic considerations. In any case, it was no easy
job to secure independence. It was a struggle, sometimes involving violence, as in Algeria, Ivory Coast,
Cameroun, Kenya, Madagascar. It was a struggle in
which the colonial government held the reins of force,
often had more outside support than their opposition
(at least at first), and claimed whatever legitimacy it
had been able to gain through the years either directly
or via the chiefs.

A nationalist movement, in order to succeed, had to
make battle for the minds of men. It had to try to
inculcate among the majority of the people resident in
a territory a system of values and norms that was often
at direct variance with that of the legal government.
Above all, it had to make the majority respond to its
sanctions rather than to those of the colonial government.

To accomplish this, the nationalist movement had to

do more than just establish a political party. It tried to
create around the political party a whole network of affiliated or linked organizations—youth groups, women's
groups, ex-servicemen's groups, trade unions, farmers'
associations, ethnic associations, friendly societies,
separatist churches. In some cases the nationalist
movement took over existing voluntary associations. In
other cases it created new ones. But in all cases its
purpose was to inculcate large numbers of persons with
new (revolutionary) values and norms. The nationalist
movement sought to corral all the leisure time of the
individual, so that wherever he went, whatever he did,
he would find himself in an environment which reinforced these new beliefs. Thus arose the cry for the
primacy of political values, the politicization of all
activity, at least until independence was won.

The reaction of the colonial government to this
argument was the counterargument of "apoliticism,"
the argument that voluntary organizations should not
be diverted or divided by politics. But talk of diversion
cut both ways, and the nationalist movement asserted
that apolitical leisure activity was a deliberate lure and
diversion created by the colonial government to distract
people from the central issue, the struggle for independence. Thus, one of the key fights came to be the
fight to control the voluntary associations, a fight that
in the long run was won by the nationalist movement.

When this fight was substantially won, when the
party had organized itself throughout a territory, when
the party had given political interpretation to the
manifold grievances of the population, when, therefore,
the majority of the people shifted their passive alle-
giance from the colonial powers and the traditional
chiefs to the mass nationalist movement, a "time of
troubles" began. Once this happened, the colonial
powers sought to come to terms with the nationalist
movement in order to establish an orderly (that is, as
slow as politically possible) transition. Taking into

account the changing world situation and particularly
the emergence of the Bandung spirit, the colonial
powers acted with great speed in the nonsettler territories, particularly in West and Equatorial Africa.
There seemed no virtue in resisting some transfer of
power once the nationalist movement showed itself in
relative command of the loyalties of the majority of the
population. This was not true in the settler territories
(Algeria and southern Africa) where the pressures of
the white settler population and the often important
economic interests of the colonial power meant both
that it was harder to organize the nationalist movement
and that a longer "time of troubles" was required once
it had begun.

But sooner or later this era came to an end. The
colonial powers—first Britain, then France, then
Belgium—decided to move ahead, devolving power
upon the nationalist movement as a step (sometimes
only implicitly) toward full independence. And so for
an interim period, the colonial government and the
nationalist movement shared power; there was, in
short, a dyarchy. How long this existed varied according to the situation in a given territory. Generally
speaking, the longer a colonial power waited to begin
the transfer of power, the shorter the period of dyarchy
was. Compare the French Congo and the Belgian
Congo, or British West Africa and French West Africa.
And generally speaking, the longer the period of dyarchy, the smoother the transition. This was so not
only because more Africans received training to man
the administration, but because the political structures
that Africans created gave them the sense of control
over their own destinies, thus minimizing psychological
resentment against the former colonial power.

A long period of shared power also had the effect of
moderating the promises that the nationalist movement
made to its constituency since the taste of power
brought a sobering sense of proportion to the analyses

of political decisions. On the other hand, a long transition placed the nationalist movement in an ambivalent position, in which it often lost support precisely because it became more "moderate." The resulting disaffection of intellectuals and young people often changed the nature of the movement.

But the differences between the long and short periods of transition were not too great. We are talking of a variation that ranges from one year or so (say, the Congo) to nine years or so (say, Nigeria). It is an important variation but, in the long perspective of history, it would be unwise to exaggerate its importance.

Eventually, no matter how often the colonial power in a particular colony denied that independence would result from the political changes, independence was gained. And with independence, the nature of the problems facing the governments of African nations—the former nationalist movements which now came to power—changed radically. But before discussing the postindependence era, it would be well to retrace our steps a bit, to review the history of the colonial era in Africa not in terms of the general pattern that was followed everywhere, but rather with emphasis on the differences between colonial powers and differences in developments in various regions.

:IV:

THE DIFFERENT

EUROPEAN LEGACIES

African nationalism did not follow an identical path everywhere for a number of reasons. There were several colonial powers, and they engaged in different practices even within their own territories. Some territories had settlers and others not. Some got their independence early and others late. Some achieved it by violence; some succeeded without violence; a few had their independence handed to them in the wake of others. Arab Africa was in some respects unlike black Africa. The existence of a third grouping (Indians, Coloureds, etc.) sometimes made a difference.

We have seen that although Britain and France had dabbled on the edge of Africa for a long time and even established a few colonies, the period of their greatest imperialist expansion was the last quarter of the nineteenth century. This was the moment of Belgian and German colonization as well. (The Portuguese expanded in those places where they already had been for centuries.) At this point in European history, all these colonizing powers shared one ideological assumption—the supremacy of the values of Western civilization and the moral duty of the West to impose at least some of

these values on Africa. There was, in short, a basic
element of paternalism which ran through the philoso-
phies of all the colonial powers. But this basic paternalism expressed itself in very different forms, depending
on the history and national character of the colonial
powers.

From the beginning, there was a sparseness and
economy about British colonial policy. The British, of
course, had started by using private companies as the
mechanism of acquisition, and even later the British
would justify the acquisition of a new colony largely on
the basis of its economic return. The middle of the
nineteenth century saw a political battle in England in
which one powerful faction wished to abandon British
colonies (including the Gold Coast) on the grounds that
they were not worth holding. British colonies were always required to be self-financing, a fact which made it
difficult for the colonial administration to pay for basic
public works. And since the constitutional structure of
Britain itself was one of complex variation, the British
saw no difficulty in varying the structure of each of its
colonies, according to the immediate needs of the situation. This policy was typical of the famous British
pragmatism.

The men who go overseas for an imperial power often
are romantics. In British areas these men got more lee-
way than in other colonies, often because they were the
only ones really interested in colonial policy. The
romantics among the soldiers teamed up with the
romantics among the anthropologists, and it may be
said that out of this union emerged the famous policy
of "indirect rule," the policy of allowing the powers of
traditional rulers to remain intact to the maximum
degree consonant with imperial rule. Though Lord
Lugard, when he initiated this policy in Northern
Nigeria, may have had in mind primarily the fact that
he had an inadequate number of soldiers and administrators to govern such a large region directly, the exten-

sion of the policy elsewhere and its emergence as an ideology can be traced to the responsive note it touched in British hearts.

Though the British may have felt it their duty to accept the "white man's burden" and bear the responsibility of advancing African interests, they did not assume that Africa one day would be an extension of Britain, or Africans one day British. The bias of the administrator—and more importantly, of the Briton at home—was in favor of the traditional chief in colonial government and not the Oxford-trained lawyer, who was felt to be somehow out of place. In short, British paternalism took the form of pressures to preserve custom, to maintain distance between Britain and Africa, between Briton and African.

The paternalism of France took a very different form. There was a Jacobin tradition in addition to that of aristocratic romance. During the French Revolution (An II Pluviôse), and again in the first flush of the Second Republic, in 1848, France granted full rights of citizenship to the inhabitants of the four communes of Senegal, including the right to send a deputy to the parliament of France. It was a lordly gift, that of human rights, of fraternal participation, in the land of freedom and culture.

There was no preference here for primitive chiefs. The *évolué*, graduate of a French university, denizen of a Paris salon, the African who had thoroughly imbibed French culture was the man to be honored. This is what was meant by "assimilation." In 1946 France would boast that the official grammarian of the Constitutional Convention was an African *agrégé*, Léopold Senghor. Neither distance nor racism here; the cultivated African was a deputy of France.

This Jacobin egalitarianism blended very well with the attempt of the French right wing in the late nineteenth century to restore the country to its former glory. Smarting over the defeat of 1870–71, Jules Ferry led France to seek some compensation in an overseas empire. There was no counting of pennies, no gross economic justification for expansion in this case. Nor did each territory suffice unto itself, economically and administratively. The French tradition of centralization and of consistent logic, applied to the needs of empire building, imposed standardized patterns throughout French colonies; the personnel were interchangeable and the curricula of the schools—all of them in French —were alike.

This, then, is the classic contrast between Africa's two colonial powers, Britain and France: Britain— empirical, commercial, practicing indirect rule, keeping Africans at a distance, verging on racism; France— Cartesian in its logic, seeking glory, practicing direct administration, acting as apostle of fraternity and anti-racism. Anyone who travels in both British and French Africa will see the grain of truth in these generalizations. The flavor of life *is* different; the two colonial powers *have* produced two different cultures. And yet, anyone who travels there well knows the severe limitations of these generalizations.

It is true that the British made a virtue of indirect rule and the French of direct administration. But what Lugard invented for Northern Nigeria and Sir Donald Cameron adapted for Tanganyika, Marshal Lyautey also practiced and preached in Morocco. The French may have ignored many chiefs, but if they were suffi-ciently powerful, as the Moro Naba in Upper Volta or the Lamidos in northern Cameroun, they had a better chance of surviving with customs and powers little changed than many petty chieftains in the coastal areas of British West Africa.

As for "empiricism" versus "Cartesian logic," this comparison smacks more of slogans than of analysis. For if the British permitted much variation, they also established clear patterns for their system of colonial administration, as well as for the political devolution that occurred later. If Cartesian logic led the French to such "strange" steps as granting identical constitutional reforms in 1956 to thirteen African territories, the logic of political wisdom led them to have a different real policy toward each of these thirteen territories. The reality of power did not always match the judicial format.

To contrast motives of money and glory seems even more dubious. For the British were surely proud of their empire, and the French surely profited by theirs. As for "racism" and "fraternity," it may be that French paternalism was based on the exclusive virtue but universal accessibility of French civilization and British paternalism on the equal virtue of all traditions but the unique inaccessibility of British culture. Nevertheless, in practice, there were parallel degrees of political, social and economic discrimination in two settler territories like Kenya and Algeria, and there were parallel ideologies among the settlers. There was also parallel absence of legal discrimination in nonsettler British and French West Africa, though until 1957 the exclusive white clubs of both areas barred Africans as members or as guests.

Having examined some of the differences and similarities between British and French colonial rule, let us now look at the colonial ideologies of the two other major powers whose legacies matter, Belgium and Portugal.

The Congo has a peculiar colonial history. In the late nineteenth-century scramble for Africa, the Congo Free State came into existence. This was a country run by a private corporation presided over by King Leopold of Belgium as a private individual. In the short period of twenty years, the Congo Free State managed to concentrate so many of the horrors of colonialism (vast exploitation by means of forced labor and chopped-off hands) that an international scandal was caused. In the wake of this scandal, the administration was turned

over to the Belgian government, who were absolutely
determined to wipe out the very memory of the scandal.
The Congo became a "model" colony—more hospitals
and more primary school education than in any other
colony in Africa (except perhaps the Union of South
Africa). But to avoid trouble the government would
also brook no opposition, allow no one political rights,
either settler or African. And in order to be sure that
no African would demand them, there would be no
elites—much primary education but almost no secondary education, and no university education at all.
Nowhere did "papa know better" than in the Congo;
nowhere did more sanitary bliss reign.

Only Portuguese paternalism can claim to rival the
Belgian variety. Portugal's great colonial era had been
the sixteenth century. By the nineteenth and twentieth
centuries, Portugal was very tired. And its African
colonies were very sleepy—forced labor, a few churches,
and an occasional intermarriage (more occasional as the
years went by). Neither Angola nor Mozambique was a
"model" colony. When Salazar took over Portugal, the
rights he denied to Portuguese he was not prepared to
extend to Africans. And so a tight lid was kept on, as in
the Congo—not because, as in the Congo, it was feared
that otherwise matters would explode and call down
international wrath once again, but because a tight lid
was the normal state of affairs. Belgium and Portugal
did share an "assimilationist" bias with France in that
each had a system of permitting individual Africans to
attain full legal rights by passing a test proving they
had surmounted the cultural barrier. But neither
Belgium nor Portugal was as close to Britain as France
was in terms of permitting some limited political organization by the Africans. This difference would prove
to be crucial.

As a result of their special framework of thinking
concerning the colonies, the British were the first to
begin the process of decolonization. Their attitude

could be traced in part to their unhappy experiences in British North America. Having suffered the American Revolution, the British sought to avoid a repetition in Canada and thus began to consider how to devolve powers on the colonists, and how to do it before an explosion occurred. The British tradition of local government plus the fact that the people to whom these powers were at first transferred were largely Englishmen (Canada, Australia, New Zealand) made decolonization a relatively painless procedure.

In the middle of the nineteenth century, legislative bodies on which local people served were created in British colonies in Africa. Thus, the political experience of British West Africans, experience in modern parliamentary government, had a long history and would come to serve this area well. By the same token, in the settler areas of southern Africa, the British also created local legislative bodies, but here the power went in part to white settlers. As these white settlers got more and more autonomy, they eliminated African participation in government, at least until a much later stage of African nationalism. This was the history notably of the Union of South Africa. After the Boer War, the British were generous in their willingness to turn back power to the population of South Africa: the Boers were given coequal rights with the English colonists, but there were suffrage rights and parliamentary representation for Coloureds and Africans as well. When Britain went all the way and granted independence to the Union of South Africa, the dominant white population began to eliminate first the Africans, then the Coloureds, from any political role. Similarly, in Southern Rhodesia the white settlers received substantial autonomy, and in Kenya they received some, for a long time to the detriment of African participation in government.

The British acceptance of the devolution of powers, of the legitimacy of the objective of national independ-

ence, led to a situation in which African nationalism
could flourish in West Africa and white settler nationalism could flourish in East, Central, and South Africa,
until African nationalism caught up with the latter and
began to force a rethinking of the political situation,
both by the settlers and by the British government.
What should be underlined here is that autonomous
development, the ultimate acquisition of independence,
were always considered reasonable, indeed inevitable,
objectives of British colonies in Africa. Once Britain
had expanded her previously white Commonwealth
after the Second World War to include the Asian
dominions of India, Pakistan and Ceylon, there seemed
no reason why African countries, first of all the Gold
Coast and Nigeria,* should not proceed along this
path. Thus, the pace of constitutional development in
British nonsettler Africa was rapid and marked by a
minimum of violence and antagonism. The rapid transfer of power here was to serve as the model and impetus
for it elsewhere in Africa.

The French had experienced no early colonial revolt
such as the American Revolution leading to the development of a white Commonwealth whose structure
could be extended later to nonwhite nations. The
French concept of constitutional advance was to draw
colonies closer to France, not push them farther away.
The Second World War forced France as well as Britain
to reconsider its colonial policy. For one thing, the Free
French movement had received early support in black
Africa,† and after the war, therefore, the government
thought that such loyalty deserved to be rewarded.

* The same logic, at the same time, applied to the Sudan,
except that this country, having been a condominium with Egypt,
did not remain within the Commonwealth after independence.

† French black Africa is a term that has been used to include
what were formerly the eight territories of French West Africa,
the four of French Equatorial Africa, and the trust territories of
Togo and Cameroun. All fourteen territories are now independent
states.

Thus, in 1944, General de Gaulle convened a conference
on colonial affairs in Brazzaville calling for great reforms. In his very famous opening speech to this conference, René Pléven, then Minister of Colonies,
pledged new institutions and added: "There are populations that we intend to lead, step by step, to a more
complete personality, to political enfranchisement, but
who do not expect to know an independence other than
the independence of France." Consequently, the major
constitutional reform of this period was the fact that
French African territories were to elect members to all
of France's legislative bodies. As constitutional advance
in British West Africa from 1946 to 1956 meant allowing more and more Africans to participate in the local
legislature and executive, so in French Africa it meant
allowing more and more Africans to participate in
France's legislature and executive.

The French concept of illegitimacy of independence
meant not only that the constitutional patterns were
different from the British but also that the organizational patterns were different. African political parties
were sometimes mere extensions of metropolitan parties (such as the SFIO in Senegal). But even if they
were not, the fact that they had elected members in
France's parliamentary bodies meant that, for reasons
of parliamentary survival and influence, they had to
attach themselves (*apparenter*) to a party in France
(an example was the attachment of the RDA* to the
French Communist Party, and later, when it broke
with the Communist Party, to the center UDSR party).
More important even than this political attachment
was the fact that various kinds of nonpolitical associations were also organized as branches of French organizations. This was true of everything from boy scouts
to war veterans, but it was most significant in the case
of trade unions; for a long time all African trade unions

* Rassemblement Démocratique Africain, a party organized
in most territories of French black Africa.

were part of the three French federations, the CGT,
the CFTC, and the Force Ouvrière, particularly the
first.

The end of the Second World War saw French colonies started on a radically different path of development from that of the British colonies (that is, the
nonsettler ones). And yet, fifteen years later, they had
all arrived at approximately the same point, national
independence. What had happened to make the French
pattern begin to conform to the British pattern?

There were two principal levers that forced a shift in
the French pattern of constitutional development. One
was the example of Ghana; the other, the developments
in North Africa and Indochina. The French North
African states each had a national identity, however
limited, that predated French conquest. And although
Algeria was juridically the most assimilated of France's
African possessions, Tunisia and Morocco were the
least. They were technically "protectorates" governed
by their own rulers who had signed treaties with France.
All of French North Africa had known the beginnings
of nationalist ferment before the Second World War.
The currents of nationalism in the Arab world had
touched them, particularly Morocco. The size of the
indigenous elite, the existence of a commercial as well
as of a professional middle class, could not fail to have
some influence. So when Indochina, in its Asian sur-
roundings, pushed its claims to independence by revolution, and when Libya was handed its independence
on a platter because of Italian defeat and cold war
rivalries, Tunisia and Morocco became very restive
and demanded not more integration into France but
real devolution of power. North African trade unionists
broke with the French CGT to create their own autonomous structures, thus starting a new pattern.

French black Africa felt these new ideas of autonomism coming from North Africa. They were particularly well received in Togo and Cameroun, which as

early as 1946 were able to proclaim openly the objective of independence because of their status as trust territories. The independence of Tunisia and Morocco in 1956, the granting under United Nations pressure of some autonomy to Togo in 1955, the imminent independence of Ghana, and above all the Algerian war that had been going on since 1954, all led to the African demand for the *loi-cadre*,* which was granted in 1956. This law set French black Africa on the path to independence, which most of them obtained in 1960. The French had made the same decision as the British, to come to terms with the new urban elite; and the elite in French Africa had made the same decision as the elite in British Africa, that only independence would meet their demand for political equality. The difference was that the British had long accepted the goal of independence but the French had accepted it only very late and with the greatest difficulty.

These were not the only differences. One thing the British were very eager to export was their particular version of parliamentary government. In the process of turning over power, the British used their influence as a pressure toward the development of a multi-party system. The French did not seem to care. When the French were fighting the nationalist party, they created opposition parties; when they decided to come to terms with the nationalists, they seemed just as happy to have only a single group with which to deal. But as we shall see, after independence the pressures of the social structure toward a one-party state were more important than Britain's effort to encourage multi-party systems.

The fact that the British officially proclaimed the object of independence and the French officially rejected it caused a different attitude during the crucial period of the dyarchy on the question of creating larger polit-

* A law which gave semi-autonomy to the eight territories of French West Africa, the four of French Equatorial Africa, as well as to Madagascar and French Somaliland.

ical federations. The British worked hard and actively
toward achieving the constitutional formulae which
permitted Nigerian federalism and Ghanaian regionalism. The British also worked for East African unity.
The French officially abstained from, unofficially
worked against, the achievement of federations in
French West and French Equatorial Africa, partly
because at critical moments those forces which pushed
toward federalism seemed to be pushing toward more
rapid independence, which was still anathema to the
French. Nevertheless, as we shall see again, the forces
pushing toward unitary structures within states (for
example, the breakdown of regionalism in Ghana) and
toward new ties between independent African states
were such as to eclipse the importance of the different
attitudes of the British and French during the transition period.

Another difference in heritage was the concept of the
role of the civil service. Great Britain has long placed
great emphasis on the nonpolitical role of the civil
service. Senior civil servants are forbidden to engage in
partisan political activity, even as private citizens, in
order to reinforce the norm that they impartially serve
alternating political masters. The French exclude only
the most senior group. Not only are a larger number of
positions in a ministry overtly political (*le cabinet privé
du ministre*) but most permanent civil servants have
the rights of all other citizens in terms of active politics.
Indeed, the result is that there are clans of French civil
servants "linked" with French political tendencies—
a rarer occurrence in Britain. This difference, carried
over into Africa, was very important during the colonial
period. Since the government was the chief employer
of the elite, an African civil servant often had to choose
between keeping his job and active association with
the nationalist movement. The choice of "apoliticism"
did not make the civil servants popular with the future
leaders of their country. In French areas there was no

such conflict. The French could retaliate against a civil servant who was a nationalist by transferring him, but they could not fire him. The dichotomy between African civil servant and African political leader was therefore never as sharp. But once again, after independence, the conflicts between civil servant and politician deriving from their different interests would far outweigh the importance of the different norms that ex-British and ex-French Africans derived from their colonial heritage. In short, although the British differed from the French in terms of their attitudes toward a multi-party system, the construction of political federations, the nature and role of the civil service, these differences became less important as African nations faced the new imperatives of the postindependence era.

A more significant difference, perhaps, was the cultural heritage. I do not mean here the fact that educated British Africans drink tea and French Africans like *apéritifs*. This is true, and it is striking to the visitor as he moves from country to country; but it represents merely a difference in the thin outer veneer of the styles of life prevalent in various African countries. There is, however, a more important aspect of the difference in European cultural heritage. The French favored assimilation. All schooling was in French from the very first grade of elementary school. African politicians served in French assemblies. The British placed less emphasis on cultural assimilation. Schooling was in English only in later years. Africans in England never were absorbed into English life, as Africans in Paris were absorbed into French life.

The net result was that the French produced a much more *dépaysé* individual. Educated British Africans resumed the wearing of African dress early. It became legitimate for the most formal occasions. Literacy drives were conducted to teach people to read African languages. African intellectuals would often speak African languages among themselves if they had one in com-

mon. French African intellectuals wore European dress
on almost all occasions, and spoke French among themselves—and often their French was much better than
the English of their British African counterparts. This
greater assimilation gave rise to a greater reaction, that
of negritude, the reassertion of the cultural values not
of particular African tribes but of the Negroes as one
large cultural group. As one Nigerian expressed it,
British Africans did not need to invent the concept of
negritude, for they had been practicing it all their lives.
This difference in cultural tone, coming out of different
colonial experience, accentuated by the lack of contact
between Africans in various European colonies during
the colonial period, made a lasting impression on the
new African societies.

Did the fact of having settlers in an African colony
make a permanent difference? Clearly it made a big
difference in the pace and the forms of the struggle for
independence. Settlers meant greater passion, hatred,
violence. Settlers meant searing memories of overt
discrimination. Settlers meant Africans had fewer
opportunities before independence to obtain experience
in posts of responsibility. On the other hand, settlers
also usually meant that more Africans were involved in
the money economy, more went to primary school, and
hence more worked as clerks, typists, and the like.
Most of all, large numbers of settlers meant that the
Africans absorbed more Western values and habits
(compare Africans in the Union of South Africa with
Ghanaians, or even Algerians with Moroccans). How
many of these differences, however, are but mere tran-
sitory differences? It is far too early to tell. In the year
2000 the influence of settlers may seem an insignificant
detail or it may loom large as an explanation of varying
patterns. Its significance will depend in part on how
the transition is made from white domination to
African control in settler areas.

The main factor distinguishing the Belgian or the

Portuguese attitude toward territories from both the
British and the French attitudes was their unwilling-
ness to accept not merely the desirability but even the
conceptual possibility of independence. When the Belgians suddenly faced rebellion in the Congo, which
came in the wake of autonomy and independence for
French Equatorial Africa, in turn speeded up by the
Algerian war, they evaded the issue by pulling out
quickly to avoid a costly colonial war. Because the
Belgians had not granted political rights to the Congolese until a very late date, the transition was necessarily abrupt. The Congolese did not have time to
develop the kind of strong party structure which
enabled Africans in West or North Africa to make
similar transitions without difficulty. The effects of
this sudden transition may prove long-lasting if the
Congolese find it difficult to create sufficient national
solidarity to permit continued economic advance.

The length of time involved in the transfer of power
was important in determining the makeup and development of the newly created independent governments.
Time made possible party organization and administrative experience. The degree of resistance by the
colonial power often determined the character of political parties. Too much resistance (Congo) made it
difficult to develop a party structure; too little resulted
in a weak structure as well. This was the case, for example, of those French African countries—Chad,
Gabon—which got their independence as a result of the
struggle of the stronger ones. Also, the RDA party
structure in Guinea and Mali is tighter than in the
Ivory Coast because the French came to terms with
the RDA in the Ivory Coast in 1952 and in Guinea and
Mali only in 1956. Between 1952 and 1956, the Ivory
Coast party did not rebuild its organizational structure,
which had been weakened by repression in 1949, partly
because it did not need to.

The strength of the traditional African rulers also

determined the course of development of new governments, whether it was strength deriving from precolonial tradition or strength resulting from being favored
in the colonial situation (as, for example, those chiefs
who used the installation of cash crops to secure for
themselves a new, vital role in the money economy).
The Istiqlal Party in Morocco could not play the same
unifying role (indeed the party itself split in two after
independence) as the Neo-Destour Party in Tunisia,
in part because of strong traditional rulers, eager to
maintain their own supremacy. The strength of traditional rulers in northern Nigeria and Cameroun has
meant that the populations of the northern parts of
these countries, who are less educated than the southerners, could nevertheless have a vital influence in
national politics. Comparable groups in the northern
parts of Dahomey, Togo, Ghana, and the Ivory Coast,
where the traditional structures were less complex and
unified than in the emirates of northern Nigeria and
Cameroun, did not have such influence. Ugandan
nationalism has proved no faster than Kenyan nationalism, although Africans in Kenya had to contend with
settlers, because Uganda is beset with strong traditional
rulers who have delayed constitutional advance for fear
that it would mean their eclipse. These variations in
the strength of traditional rulers may make a long-
range difference in the patterns of African nations.

Similarities and differences in African development
in a sense depend on the perspective of the observer.
Very close up, no two African countries look alike. As
the observer recedes into the distance of space or time,
the differences too recede. Given the vast expanse of
territory, the large number of administrative divisions,
and the multiplicity of tribes which Africa knows, one
would expect the differences to appear much more
striking than they do. If they do not, it is perhaps because the transition to independence from colonial rule

has been so compressed in time—almost simultaneous for many African nations.

What is perhaps most important is the degree to which Africans themselves feel their histories are similar. We shall discuss this as part of the vision of pan-Africanism and as part of the process of cultural regeneration. We now turn from the colonial period to see the problems of the new nations after independence, the independence for which they struggled so ably and so hard.

Independence
and After

〠〠〠〠〠〠〠

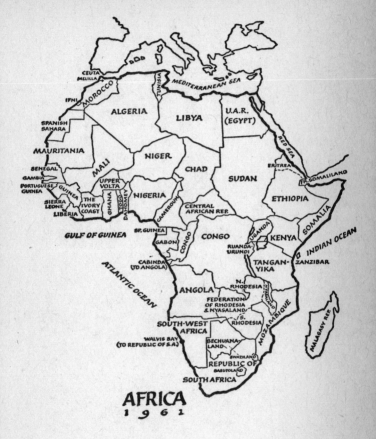

AFRICA

1 9 6 1

:V:

INTERNAL UNITY:

PARTIES AND HEROES

Independence, as the nationalists had always insisted, makes a lot of difference. It transfers much of the effective power to individuals and structures internal to the country. It gives the governing elite many levers to reclaim still more power from outside agencies. There are, however, many claimants to the exercise of this power, all internal to the country. Unless the power is effectively exercised by a central agency, and unless the rules of the power game are generally accepted by all the competitors, disintegration and secession become not merely possible but probable.

Most African nations do not have long histories as nationalities. Their nationhood has been created in the crucible of a revolutionary struggle against a colonial power. The unity of the nation was forged in the fight against the external enemy. We have sought to explain how it was that colonial governments bred their own dissolution, how nationalism came about as a resolution of many of the basic strains of the colonial situation. The question we must now address ourselves to is the opposite one. It is not how a social conflict can emerge out of a seemingly stable regime but rather how social order can emerge out of a seemingly unstable regime.

The government of a new nation, immediately after independence, is a very unstable thing. For one thing, the existence of an external enemy—the major motivation for unity in the nationalist movement—has largely disappeared. The political mobilization, the subordination of private and sectional claims to the needs of the whole, is inevitably diminished. The country's sense of tension, and of antagonism, is partly abated, partly turned inward. Moreover, there is a sense of disappointment at unfulfilled expectations.

In nationalist activity in Africa there was an implicit promise that the tension resulting from oppression and antagonism, from the restraints of the colonial ruler and from the discipline of the nationalist organization would be temporary. There was a touch of the utopian hope characteristic of every revolution, even when nationalist movements were peaceful and unmilitant, as they were in perhaps half the African states that gained independence. And there were many in all African states who thought that freedom meant the end of social control or the immediate radical redistribution of wealth. The cadres of the nationalist parties may not have had such naïve expectations, but it is understandable that among the peasants or uneducated urban dwellers such illusions existed. Even if these illusions were only momentary, unfulfillment meant a sense of disappointment. Independence was not magic. In country after country in Africa, during the first weeks of independence, the leaders felt the need to make speeches on the theme that independence means hard work and self-reliance.

Even leaving aside simplistic notions, the transfer of power inevitably involves some administrative confusion. In those countries where the transfer was abrupt, as in Guinea, the problem was much greater than in those where the transfer was meticulously planned, as in Ghana or Nigeria. Nonetheless, wherever transfer of

power occurs, it means some changes in personnel and
in formal rules. Temporarily the population feels
unsure of the rules governing behavior, and more particularly, of the limits of possible deviance. Whenever
this happens, people will test the limits, see how far
they can go. And how far they can go depends not only
on the rules, formal and informal, but on the people
who enforce the rules. To the extent that the people in
power are new and inexperienced, they may be either
too rigid or too weak-kneed in their interpretations;
they may either provoke unnecessary antagonism toward the government or allow too much license—or
often do both at once. This commonplace situation is
one of the problems that have been called the "infantile
maladies of independence."

The removal of the prod to unity—that is, colonial
rule—combined with the uncertainty, disillusion, and
hence opposition, created by the new government,
inevitably causes the ethnic, regional, and other particular interests which had temporarily held back their
claims to reassert them. This, of course, is not startling.
The assertion of the rights of private interests to their
share of the community's assets is the daily business of
all governments, not only those in Africa. What is different in new nations is that the government cannot
assume a residual loyalty to the state among the
majority of its citizens.

Loyalty to the state can be measured by the sense of
restraint its citizens feel in pursuing their opposition to
specific policies of the government. If they oppose the
particular government in power but stop at a point
short of destroying the state or seriously weakening it,
they can be said to be loyal. This kind of legitimation
of the state rather than of a particular government is
something that is inculcated in the population over a
period of time. Children are taught it in schools. But
African nations have not yet had time for this. At
present many Africans cannot determine the limits of

opposition, do not understand the distinction between opposition and secession. This is what leaders of African governments mean when they argue that "our oppositions are not constructive." It is not that they tend to be destructive of the government in power; this is the purpose of an opposition. It is that they tend to destroy the state in the process of trying to depose the acting government.

This is particularly true because, in almost every African country, the opposition takes the form of a claim to regionalism—a demand for at least decentralization in a unitary state, federalism in a decentralized state, confederation in a federation, total dissolution of a confederation. Regionalism is understandable because ethnic loyalties can usually find expression in geographical terms. Inevitably, some regions will be richer (less poor) than others, and if the ethnic claim to power combines with relative wealth, the case for secession is strong. Ashanti in Ghana, the Ivory Coast in French West Africa, the Western Region in Nigeria, Gabon in French Equatorial Africa, Katanga in the Congo are all well-known examples. But every African nation, large or small, federal or unitary, has its Katanga. Once the logic of secession is admitted, there is no end except in anarchy. And so every African government knows that its first problem is how to hold the country together when it is threatened by wide disintegration.

The integration of a country can be assured in the long run only if the majority of the citizens begin to accept the state as the legitimate holder of force and authority, the rightful locus of legislation and social decision. President Senghor of Senegal has pointed out that: "In Africa, the Fatherland [*patrie*] is the *Serer* country, the *Malinke* country, the *Sonhrai*, the *Mossi*, the *Baule*, the *Fon* country. The Nation unites Fatherlands in order to transcend them. It is not, like the Fatherland, a natural phenomenon, therefore an ex-

pression of the milieu, but a will to construct or rather
to reconstruct. . . . In order to achieve its object, the
Nation must inspire all its members, all its individuals
to seek in it, beyond their Fatherlands, their faith."

If this faith is weak, if citizens tend regularly to
question not only the wisdom of the government's acts
but its very right to engage in these acts, what can
those who are interested in creating a nation do to
enhance this acceptance, to diminish this questioning
of the very basis of authority? This is not an abstract
question; it has been the most urgent question that the
government of every newly independent African nation
has asked itself. And not surprisingly, most of them
have come up with a similar series of answers, sugges-
tions for ways in which they can work to create the
bases of stable government.

What are these answers? One problem of new African
nations is that they are new. People are not used to
them. People cannot tell themselves that the ways of
the state are hallowed by tradition, justified by experience. Even a modern rational state depends in part on
its tradition (Britain on its unwritten constitution,
France on its revolution or revolutions, the United
States on its Founding Fathers and their views) to
reinforce its legal structure. But tradition is in any
case, and anywhere, largely myth. It exists in the minds
of men. And if it is not there already, tradition can be
created or re-created, revived and installed. And so in
countless ways, African nations are today reëmphasiz-
ing their links with the past, their historical roots and
glories, their cultural achievements, their unique
virtues. Thus, Nigeria will invest in archaeological research, Senegal will sponsor a Festival of African Culture, and Morocco will recall the glories of the Almo-
ravid Empire. Every state will build museums and
encourage its historians to review and revive its past.
We shall discuss this phenomenon in detail when we
talk of cultural revival. Let us just note here that one

of the immediate results of such emphasis on tradition is that it leads to a greater legitimation of the state.

To build a nation, it is not enough to have a past. One must have a present. To the extent that the various parts of a country are economically interdependent, to the extent that specialization proceeds and division of labor occurs within national boundaries, it becomes difficult, or rather expensive, to "secede." It is no accident that immediately after independence, customs and immigration barriers suddenly become tighter, as for example between Ghana and Togo, or between Guinea and Sierra Leone. There are many reasons for such a development, but one is that it fosters the creation of a *national* economy, which among other things reinforces the sense of nationhood and hence the basic loyalty of the citizens.

Before an African colony achieves independence it is part of an imperial economy. The shift to a national economy after independence is sometimes only a partial one, though the new government may try to intensify it for political rather than economic reasons. The expansion of the road and rail network, the diversification of agriculture, the building of dams and the spread of light industries—all of which have such a high priority in the newly independent African countries—serve many economic functions. They serve as well, however, to make less likely, more difficult, any weakening of the political bonds. The desperate hurry of African leaders for economic development is due not only to the desire for a higher standard of living and the need to fulfill their promises on this front, but also to the sheer political need to hold a unit together. Economic development does this both by showing that the nation works, and by enlarging the penalties of disintegration of the state. The changes in the economy thus affect the psychological attitude of the population toward the state.

Greater functional interdependence, then, leads to

greater integration, because as movements grow up
which pull the state apart they come to see more and
more the disadvantages of their own disruptive processes. The earlier they see this, the steadier will be the
path of government. For functional interdependence
leads to greater integration only if the citizens are aware
of how interdependent they have become. The nation
and its economic network must become "visible." And
whether what is visible is reality or an inflated reality
is rather irrelevant in terms of its effect in enhancing
the loyalty of the citizens; hence, the very great importance of public relations—what is pejoratively
known as propaganda. So everywhere in independent
Africa we see an immediate creation or expansion of
the government information service, of a radio station,
of official newspapers. It is not merely for international
prestige that Nigeria or Tunisia, Mali or Ghana puts
loudspeakers in every village. It is for the sake of informing large numbers of people regularly that the
nation is not merely an invention of remote intellectuals
but something whose structure affects their lives and
economic well-being intimately and increasingly. Perhaps even more than for the sake of informing people,
it is for convincing them.

The legitimation of which we speak, the citizens'
sense of loyalty to the nation, is best tested by the willingness of the average person, in the daily events of life,
to promote the enforcement of the laws, customs and
mores of the state. To some extent it is a question of
their thinking of the state as "we" and not as "they."
If the punishment for deviation must always await the
presence of the policeman, the state will not function
very well. To be sure, formal punishment is important,
and every new African state is eager to ensure that it
has at its disposition an adequate army and police
force which will be entirely loyal to it. However, government control of the army and police force is not
enough. The people must be willing to recognize the

authority of the law enforcement agencies and the government controlling them.

In the colonial situation, African national movements had taught their followers to think of the (colonial) state as "they," not "we." Independence demands a rapid reversal in outlook from opposition to support of the state's authority. This transition is difficult even for the educated and trained cadres of the movement. In Senegal or Guinea or Togo we find the newly independent governments inveighing against bureaucrats who have not learned that "sabotage" is no longer a legitimate tool of argument, that the anarchy which nationalists had demanded before had now become archaic and dangerous. To teach the uneducated majority the meaning of the law, rigorous enforcement with harsh penalties is often instituted. Immediately after independence, there are new and tighter laws governing traffic accidents, theft, murder. The new governments intend to show that they are there and that their laws are to be respected.

But the new governments must also create a climate in which laws are obeyed even in the absence of a regulatory force. The government has to teach people the rules; it has to accustom them to obeying rules. Campaigns are undertaken to induce people to report offenders, no matter how highly placed they are. Ritualized mass activities often are initiated. Americans know the "I Am An American Day" ceremonials which are used to habituate immigrants to American ways. Similar emphasis is being placed on respect for the flag and other national symbols in Africa today, especially among school children. Everywhere in independent Africa programs of "human investment" are being undertaken. The names of the programs may differ in Senegal or the Central African Republic, in Cameroun or Niger, but essentially they all call for the same thing —unpaid labor in the service of the nation. The programs are nowhere compulsory, but everywhere the

social pressure to participate is very heavy. Of course
the economic value of such activity is obvious. It
should also be observed, however, that such "noncom-
pulsory" programs rather forcibly recruit peasants and
uneducated urbanites for a *national* activity, one of
whose objects is to reiterate the norms of the nation
and encourage all the participants to punish the de-
viants by social disapproval of nonparticipation. In
Morocco, in 1957, the road built by voluntary labor
was called "The Road of Unity." Ben Barka, the
Moroccan political leader, said of this road: "It involved transforming these 'volunteers' who divided
their time on the Road between work and civic training
into truly *militant citizens*."

In speaking of the activities to enhance the integrity
of the new African states we have referred somewhat
loosely to the "nation" as undertaking these activities.
But who exactly is it that does this "enhancing?" To
some extent it is the government, and we have mentioned various governmental activities. But, as we
have seen, the government rests on weak ground because of the shallow loyalty of its citizens. The problem
of establishing the integrity of the state is precisely
that of strengthening the hand of the state machinery,
but the government itself is not necessarily the best
agent for this. The government lacks personnel and
money. Even more important, it lacks the support of
citizens with that diffuse sense of attachment, "loyalty,"
which would encourage them to promote its well-being
without being paid. The dilemma is that the government lacks people with the loyalty to undertake activities which would enhance this very "loyalty" to the
government.

Since the government cannot perform the functions
necessary for increasing its own integrity, the modernizing elite, which is in control of most of the newly independent African nations, looks around for integrating
institutions, mechanisms which are intermediate be-

tween the citizen and the state but national in orientation, mechanisms which can attract the necessary loyalty more rapidly and turn this loyalty to the service of the nation. There are, unfortunately, very few such institutions available in these new nations. Functional organizations (trade unions, students' groups, etc.), while often national in orientation, tend to represent very limited portions of the population, given the degree of economic development in these countries. National churches such as those which served to support nationalism in Europe do not usually exist. The army may occasionally be able to fill this function, but it is generally weak and its usefulness limited. Two major instruments of integration tend to emerge from the nationalist struggle for independence: the nationalist party, and the national hero. The major hope for the modernizing elite lies with these. Let us see first what is expected of these "integrating institutions," and then by what means they try to fulfill these expectations.

For one thing, they must teach the new norms, by example and by precept, by repetition and by sanction. They must teach not only sets of rules and expectations but ways of looking at the world, *national* ways. They must educate people to understand why troops should be sent to the Congo, why diseased cocoa trees must be uprooted, and why government salaries cannot constantly rise. Unless this education is undertaken, it will be difficult to enlist the energies of the population in the service of the nation.

These institutions must somehow make the citizens aware of the nation as an economic entity, of the impact of economic acts on various parts of the country, of the degree to which the peasant relies on the port worker. They have to continue to stimulate the movement of people from the villages to the towns and mines, and, for the individual, they have to serve as a tangible institution on which he can rely for help, for

advice, for consolation. These are large tasks, and the
party and the national hero do not do them alone. But
as one surveys the African scene today, one observes
that where the party and the hero are weak, so are the
processes of modernization and integration of the
nation. For in this transition to a social order in which
the state will be able to rely on the loyalty of a citizenry
born to it and trained in it, the party and the hero can
be seen somewhat as a pair of surgical clamps which
hold the state together while the bonds of affection and
legitimation grow. If one may pursue the analogy,
these bonds may grow even without the clamps, but
without them the process is more arduous and painful,
and the outcome doubtful.

We speak of *the party*, but are there not *parties*? There
are in some countries. Most African nations came to
independence by organizing a nationalist movement
which laid effective claim to power. The standard
pattern was the existence of one major party which
symbolized the struggle for independence, with some
weak, often regionalist, opposition parties. Ghana,
Togo, Sierra Leone, Somalia are examples of this. In
some few cases, as a result of either absorption or suppression, the opposition totally ceased to exist before
independence—notably in the Ivory Coast, the Republic of Mali, Tunisia; or it expired soon after independence—as in Guinea and Upper Volta. Where there was
no one party which commanded overwhelming support
—the Congo, Sudan, Nigeria—or where the nationalist
party split after independence, as in Morocco, there
often was considerable trouble. Where a major segment
of the nationalist movement was systematically excluded from power, as in Cameroun, there was continued civil war. Almost everywhere, the trend after
independence has been in one of two directions: toward
a one-party state with consequent stability (if the
resulting single party grouped the major elements) or

toward a breakdown of the party system with consequent instability and a tendency for the army to play a growing role (Sudan, Morocco, Congo).

The choice has not been between one-party and multi-party states; it has been between one-party states and either anarchy or military regimes or various combinations of the two. The military regime, beset by internal troubles, finds it difficult to mobilize energies for economic development, to keep the intellectuals satisfied and in line, to allow for participation in government by any factions other than the small ruling group. On the contrary, the single-party state—at least the single-party state where the party structure is well articulated and really functioning—provides a mechanism whereby the majority of the population can have some regular, meaningful connection with, and influence upon, the governmental process, and vice versa.

Since "single-party systems" seem to be a standard feature of the new African nations, it is well to distinguish them from the "single-party systems" in Eastern Europe, for example. The party in Africa, heir of the nationalist movement, is first of all a mass party, at least in theory. It seeks to enroll all the citizenry in its branches, including its women's and youth sections. In those nations where the party is an effective and real one, the sections meet on a regular basis, often weekly, in every village and town ward. Because almost the whole population belongs to the party, these meetings resemble "town meetings." The function of the meetings is twofold. They are arenas whereby the government via the party cadres can transmit new ideas, new projects, new demands for sacrifices—that is, they function to educate the population, so that government decisions do not remain dead letters but are really carried out. But they also serve to communicate the ideas of the people to the government as well; they are a direct channel of complaint and suggestion through which the government can be made sensitive to the

internal realities of the nation and flexible in the means
it uses to achieve its goals. There seems to be considerable evidence that this two-way process is not a sham,
or in any sense based on terror, but that it works fairly
well. Of course it works better in some places than in
others. Tunisia, Mali, Guinea, Tanganyika are models
of single-party states with two-way communication.
Ghana, Togo and the Central African Republic run
close behind. Some party structures place less emphasis
on participation, using more nebulous antennae to
remain sensitive to popular will. In these cases, the
pipe lines transmitting points of view—both upward
and downward—sometimes get clogged. The Ivory
Coast is a prime example of this, and Ivory Coast
leaders often discuss the need to revitalize the party
structure in order to bring it into line with parties of
other countries providing more active communication.

Along with such a structure goes an ideology which
argues that the party incarnates the nation, not because
it is in tune with historical destiny, but because of its
past and present accomplishments. In the past, it
fought for freedom and helped to create a national consciousness. And in the present, it is a mass, not a class,
party. If it is not a class party, it is even less an elite
party. (This is, of course, a fundamental theoretical difference between African parties and Communist parties
in Eastern Europe.) It is a party to which everyone is
encouraged to adhere, and to which the majority do
adhere.

This ideology is the basis of justification for the theory
of parallel authority—the matching of each governmental structure (national, regional, local) with a party
structure, priority always being assigned to the political
over the administrative structure. It is considered the
essence of popular control over government in Ghana
and the Ivory Coast, Niger and Tanganyika, that the
Political Bureau of the party should take precedence
over the Cabinet. The party should run the govern-

ment, not vice versa, because the party, not the government, is the emanation of the people, that is, holds their loyalty and ties them to the state. The party integrates the nation and allows the integration to be accomplished by a method that maximizes the opportunity of every citizen to participate on a regular and meaningful basis in the decision-making process. In practice small elites may still run the show, but they do so to a lesser degree than if there were no party structure.

The party is not alone, however, in performing the integrating function. It shares the stage with its most important adjunct, the national hero. The hero, the leader, is not an isolated phenomenon. He is the leader of the party as well as of the nation. Should he break his ties with the party, he could find it difficult to survive, as we see from the decline of Messali Hadj in Algeria. Nevertheless, his power is not identical with that of the party; he has a drawing power of his own, as a potential arbiter, as a militant fighter, as one who has proved his mettle and will seek the nation's good.

The appearance of national heroes in Africa often makes outside observers uncomfortable, for the latter think of parallel strong men and "dictators" elsewhere. It is important, therefore, to see why the hero looms so large in the new African nations and what function he really fulfills.

Not all "heroes" are alike. Bourguiba of Tunisia and Nkrumah of Ghana, even Abbé Fulbert Youlou in the Congo (Brazzaville) represent one style—flamboyant, triumphant, evangelizing. Sékou Touré of Guinea, Modibo Keita of Mali, even Azikiwe of Nigeria, perhaps Nyerere of Tanganyika represent another style—calculating, militant, analytical. Olympio of Togo, Houphouet-Boigny of the Ivory Coast, even Senghor of Senegal and Ferhat Abbas of Algeria represent a third style—more cautious, sure-footed, quiet. These styles may make a lot of difference in the history of pan-Africanism. They make less difference internally. The

functions of the hero at home are everywhere substantially the same. The methods employed are similar.

The role of the hero is first of all to be a readily
available, easily understood, symbol of the new nation,
someone to incarnate in his person its values and aspirations. But the hero does more than symbolize the
new nation. He legitimizes the state by ordaining obedi-
ence to its norms out of loyalty to his person. This is
what people usually mean when they speak of the
charismatic authority of these leaders.

The problem of integration is essentially one of
getting people to shift loyalty from a structure based
on tradition ("do it because it has always been done
this way") to a new artificial entity, the nation-state,
whose only justification for authority lies in its constitution ("do it because it is the rationally agreed-upon
law"). This is a new basis for authority in Africa, and
as we have seen, the majority is often reluctant to give
it much credence, particularly if there is some immediate economic or prestige advantage for not doing so—
thus "regionalism" based on "tribal," traditionalist loyalties. The charismatic justification for authority ("do
it because I, your leader, say so") can be seen as a way
of transition, an interim measure which gets people to
observe the requirements of the nation out of loyalty
to the leader while they (or their children) learn to do
it for its own sake. In short, the hero helps to bridge
the gap to a modern state. The citizens can feel an
affection for the hero which they may not have at first
for the nation. Insofar as the hero works in tandem
with a party structure, he provides a very powerful
mechanism for integration of the state. Those African
nations which have not thrown up sufficiently "heroic"
leaders clearly suffer by their absence. And since heroes
are largely made, not born, most new African nations
are doing their best to create or reinforce the image of
their hero.

The problem is keeping the special, inflated status

of the hero untarnished. The hero is a human being. He makes mistakes, antagonizes people. He often gets bad press at home as well as in other African countries and beyond Africa. He is particularly under attack by intellectuals, who resent his nonintellectual claims to authority and often his scorn for their pretensions. Actually, the hero himself may be a full-fledged intellectual (Senghor, President of Senegal and poet, Kenyatta of Kenya, an anthropologist), or at least a university graduate (Bourguiba, Nkrumah, Azikiwe, Nyerere). This does not mean that he will not find a majority of the intellectuals opposed to him or chafing under his authority. For as a national hero he represents a nonintellectual outlook. The hero must establish a national myth. The intellectual attacks national myths —though often in the name of other myths, some more local, some more universal.

Under this attack on the hero's status, the new African states have worked out a number of ways of preserving his image so that he may fulfill his function as a mediator between new citizen and new state. The most obvious way is the glorification of the hero. His name must be everywhere. Ghana has its Kwame Nkrumah Circle and the Ivory Coast its Houphouet-Boigny Bridge. Western Nigeria has its statue of Awolowo and Upper Volta its Maurice Yaméogo Stadium. Troubadors sing the praises of Bourguiba, and the late Abbé Boganda is sanctified in the Central African Republic. And there is scarcely a country where the face of the hero does not appear on stamps, where the hero does not regularly conduct triumphal tours of his country in somewhat regal style.

But if in ceremonies the hero becomes more regularly apparent after independence, in actual fact he becomes more removed—both from foreigners and from his own people. He is shielded from soiling his reputation with the day-to-day harsh situations that governments face. He is surrounded by lieutenants and associates who bear

the brunt of direct contact with the complainants, who
serve as sources of information for the hero and scape-
goats for blame. In moving about independent Africa,
one can hear the same theme song again and again.
"If only the hero knew, he would not permit it. He is
good, but the men around him do not understand us."

If all these ways of preserving the leader's authority
fail, the hero can resort to "religious" sanctification.
The Abbé Fulbert Youlou, although divested of his
sacerdotal functions by the Catholic Church, has continued to wear his cassock always. Houphouet-Boigny
would return periodically to the native village of
Yamoussoukro to meditate, and Nkrumah would go on
"spiritual retreats." The hero often allows an aura of
secrecy to build up and rumors to spread about his
consulting the imam or the marabout or the fetish
priest—any or all of them—without much regard for
his own religious affiliation.

The hero and the party, then, work together to keep
the nation unified, to hold it tightly together until the
majority of the citizens begin to internalize a degree of
loyalty to the state which will allow the government to
take this loyalty for granted. Are all African states
equally controlled by party and hero? No, obviously
not. Parties are very strong in about a quarter of the
states. These are true mass parties. There are partially
effective parties in half the states. The proportion of
genuine heroes is about the same.

There is a correlation between the strength of party
and hero and the degree of national integration and
stability. And, as we shall see, integration and stability
make possible economic development and increase the
ultimate prospects for a flexible democracy. Before we
discuss these questions, let us turn from the problem of
how to achieve or maintain internal unity in the newly
independent states to the problem of how to achieve
larger unities among African states—the whole question
of pan-Africanism.

:VI:

LARGER UNITIES:

PAN-AFRICANISM AND

REGIONAL FEDERATIONS

The drive for larger African unity, pan-Africanism, is probably stronger than similar movements elsewhere in the world. It is not strong enough to assure immediate success, perhaps not even ultimate success. But pan-Africanism seems likely to loom large as an active issue in African politics in the near future.

Pan-Africanism is a very loose term and covers several different movements, which it would be well to distinguish. Pan-Africanism may be said to have arisen first as a protest movement of American and West Indian Negroes who were reasserting their links with Africa and the achievements of African civilizations. Its precursors were the early back-to-Africa movements which led to the creation of Liberia and Sierra Leone, movements which reached their high point in the remarkable spread of Garveyism in the United States in the 1920's.

In 1919, during the Versailles Peace Conference in

Paris, the American Negro leader, W. E. B. Du Bois, organized the First Pan-African Congress, presided over by Blaise Diagne, first Negro deputy from Senegal in the French parliament. Du Bois organized four more such congresses between then and 1945, earning the title of "father of pan-Africanism." The Fifth Congress was held in Manchester in October 1945, at the end of the Second World War. Du Bois was chairman. The joint secretaries were George Padmore, West Indian Negro and latter-day theoretician of pan-Africanism, and Kwame Nkrumah. The assistant secretary was Jomo Kenyatta.

The 1945 meeting marked a shift of emphasis in pan-Africanism from a protest movement of Western hemisphere Negroes seeking racial equality, allied with African intellectuals, to a tool of African nationalist movements fighting colonial rule. One of the organizations that grew out of the Manchester meeting was the West African National Secretariat, whose secretary was Nkrumah. It was established in London in 1947. When Nkrumah was called to the Gold Coast in 1948, the Secretariat ceased to function. There were no serious organizational developments from this point until 1957, when the Gold Coast (Ghana) became independent.

Ghana's independence and the first Conference of Independent African States, held in Accra in April 1958, once more changed the character of pan-Africanism. It was still a tool in the African colonial struggle, although now a complication arose. Who would direct and control this movement? Whether independent African nations had some greater right to wield this tool than the nationalist movements in countries not yet independent would become an issue. However, as more and more African countries gained their independence, the central question became rather the unification of sovereign states.

Thus, pan-Africanism has had at least three political

objectives, which to some extent can be seen as occurring in three successive periods. First, it has been a protest movement against racism, largely of American and West Indian Negroes. In this capacity, pan-Africanism still continues. It is an interesting and important story, but we shall not tell it here. Second, pan-Africanism has been a tool in the hands of African nationalist movements struggling for independence. It probably has not been the most important tool in this struggle. It has played some role, but one far less important than internal party organization and, as a rallying force, it has been no more important than territorial nationalism. At some points, it has even caused strains and hence, perhaps, setbacks for particular nationalist movements.

Third and most recently, pan-Africanism has been a movement to establish a supranational entity or entities encompassing various independent African states—at its most hopeful, the United States of Africa. In this last aspect, pan-Africanism has perforce had only a short life, much too short for us to be able to evaluate its achievements properly. Yet in its short history, the pan-African movement has had some important successes and suffered some serious setbacks. Perhaps in reviewing these experiences we shall discern what motivations lie behind pan-Africanism and what structural factors affect its possibilities of success.

Why larger unities? On the surface, this goal seems to make little sense. We have seen how nationalist movements have struggled to create a sense of nation, to establish political and economic institutions within a national framework. Why break down this entity the moment it is set up? Yet large numbers of African politicians cry out against the "balkanization" of Africa, which they say must be overcome. For many people the slogan of the anticolonial revolution was not "independence" but "independence and unity." Ac-

cording to their standards the goal of the nationalist
movements has not been achieved by sovereignty; they
require African unity as well.

African nationalists feel that in a real sense their
struggle is an unfinished business and will continue to
be so until unity is achieved. The objective of nationalism was not independence. This was only a means—
one of two possible ones, as we have seen—to their real
goal: political equality. At one level, independence as-
sures equality in that each nation is sovereign and is
legally free to pursue its own national interest. On
another level, in the international arena, small and poor
nations are scarcely able to compete on equal terms
with big powers. Thus there appears an old political
theme: in unity there is strength. If we can achieve
African unity, it is argued, then we shall really have
control over our own society. We shall then be able to
remain apart from the quarrels of others; and we shall
then be able to obtain assistance from the outside.
This, of course, is not an irrational analysis.

The economic case for larger unities, to be sure, is
strong. It was used for a long time by colonial governments to justify the establishment of federations of
which they approved, such as the Federation of the
Rhodesias and Nyasaland. Essentially the argument is
that a larger internal market is necessary to stimulate
industrial and commercial development, and that a
larger geographical area contained within one political
framework makes for more rational economic planning.
Some claim that economic coöperation is both a justification for pan-African unity and a means through which
it can be achieved. Others oppose larger unities because
of the economic detriment to their countries (this is true
of some relatively richer countries).

Basically, though, pan-Africanism is a political (and,
as we shall see, cultural) movement. Economic arguments have proved insufficient to accomplish anything
positive. But in the political arena, the quarrels over

the pace and method of decolonization since 1957 on the one hand have destroyed some old possibilities of unity and on the other hand have created some new and unexpected channels for unity. In fact, decolonization has caused major political realignments in Africa, largely around the issues of pan-Africanism.

Colonial governments created units larger than the individual territories. Units such as French West Africa or French North Africa, British West Africa or British East Africa existed as institutional structures or at least as well-defined regions with common problems. The degree of administrative unity varied, although usually at least functional organs of coöperation existed, such as the West African Currency Board, East Africa Literature Bureau, the Institut Français d'Afrique Noire. These limited coöperative enterprises at the administrative level were matched by early nationalist groupings that were similarly organized on a regional level. Examples include the early National Congress of British West Africa, the Association des Etudiants Musulmans Nord-Africains, and most impressively, the Rassemblement Démocratique Africain, a French African political movement, at some point or other organized in what are now twelve independent countries. There were structures, then, that brought together political parties, trade unions, youth and students' groups on an interterritorial basis; but before 1957 these did not exist on an all-African basis, nor did they exist outside the framework of the colonial administrative structure, although the nationalist groups chose the widest structure available. The only all-African meeting ground before 1957 had been the pan-African congresses, and these were intermittent, inadequately representative, and without a continuing structure.

Decolonization in Africa, although occurring within a relatively short span of time, seldom occurred simultaneously in different territories, even those in the same area. Thus in British West Africa, Ghana became

independent before Nigeria which became independent
before Sierra Leone. In French West Africa, Guinea
became independent before the Federation of Mali,
which became independent before the four states of the
Conseil de l'Entente (Ivory Coast, Upper Volta, Niger
and Dahomey). Sometimes, as in French West Africa,
the very pace of decolonization became a major issue
between various African countries. The first ones to
become independent in a group of territories were reluctant to remain in joint administrative structures with
territories that were still colonies. Thus, in 1957, Ghana
withdrew from such joint enterprises as the West African Airways Corporation. After Guinea's independence
in 1958, she was excluded from the French West African
interterritorial structures, which were to disintegrate
completely by 1959. The administrative dismantling
was sometimes matched by partial collapse of the interterritorial nationalist structures during this period. This
was notably true in French black Africa. Between 1958
and 1960, as a result of quarrels over the methods of
decolonization, the integrating nationalist structures on
the party, trade union and youth levels were all seriously weakened. While Guinea and Mali and the Entente states argued over methods and immediate goals,
each was afraid to be associated with interterritorial
voluntary structures which might be of a different
political tendency than its own. So each pressed its
internal groupings to break ties with interterritorial
groups of opposite tendencies.

In British East Africa and Central Africa a different
type of dismantling of unified structures was occurring.
Here interterritorial administrative structures had come
into existence against the express wishes of the African
population and with the assent of a white settler population. This was notably the case in the establishment
of the Federation of the Rhodesias and Nyasaland
(Central African Federation) in 1953. This was also
largely true of the East African High Commission and

its correlative agencies. In both cases, African opposition to unity was based on the fear that a unification
of territories would tend to result in the prevalence
throughout the larger entity of the policies of the most
settler-dominated territory (Southern Rhodesia and
Kenya, respectively). Unity in a colonial settler context
was seen as a retrogressive step, one that would delay
rather than speed up African liberation. In East Africa,
African nationalists successfully opposed the creation
of a federal structure. In Central Africa, the primary
demand of African nationalists since 1953 has been the
dissolution of federation.

In spite of their opposition to federation in settler areas, in organizing themselves to pursue their
own aims, African nationalists have created the Pan-
African Freedom Movement of East and Central Africa
(PAFMECA) and have stated quite explicitly their
goal of a federal structure for their states, once they
have obtained independence and universal suffrage. In
1960, mindful of the experience of West African decolonization and its impact on unity, Julius Nyerere of
Tanganyika announced the willingness of his movement to accept a short delay in its then imminent
independence in order to enable Kenya and Uganda
to receive their independence simultaneously with Tanganyika. His hope was that this would enhance the
possibility of creating a single federal state.

A situation similar to that of East and Central
Africa may be seen in South Africa. There the three
so-called High Commission Territories—Basutoland,
Bechuanaland, and Swaziland—which are governed by
the United Kingdom Colonial Office, had resisted in-
corporation into the Union of South Africa, an issue
which had been discussed since 1907. In South-West
Africa, a former mandate which the Republic of South
Africa has refused to place under United Nations
trusteeship, African nationalists call for the recognition
of the trust status of the territory as a step toward

ultimate independence. Here again, as in East and
Central Africa, Africans are against unity insofar as it
means subjection to white-settler rule. The economic
arguments put forward are scorned. The political reality
is primary. On the African organizational level, however, a different picture is seen. The African nationalist
organizations of both South-West Africa and the Republic of South Africa find themselves together since
1959 in the South Africa United Front. There is very
close collaboration between the Basutoland nationalist
groups and those in the Republic.

The picture on the northeastern Horn of Africa is
somewhat different, but it also stresses the significance
of the timing of independence. In this region live the
Somali people, who during the colonial era were found
in five areas: Italian Somaliland, British Somaliland,
the southern half of French Somaliland, the Ogaden
district in eastern Ethiopia, and the northeast corner
of Kenya. There has long been a pan-Somali movement
to unite this people. The largest single group is found
in Somalia, which was Italian Somaliland, an Italian
trust territory which long in advance was promised its
independence in 1960 by the United Nations. When
the date of independence approached, the United Kingdom responded to pressure in British Somaliland by
granting this territory independence four days before
Somalia, with the express expectation that the two
would merge, which they did.

Still another variant occurred in North Africa, the
Maghreb. Here Tunisia and Morocco received their
independence in 1956, while Algeria was still fighting
for hers. The long struggle of Algeria strengthened the
moves for Maghreb unity, as various attempts were
made by independent Tunisia and Morocco to assist
Algeria. At an early point in the struggle, Tunisia's
Bourguiba proposed to France that Tunisia (and Morocco) should retrocede some of their sovereign powers
to a new French-North African confederation, provided

that Algeria first was allowed to enter on an equal
basis into a North African federation. Here is the same
simultaneity principle advocated by Nyerere in East
Africa, applied to somewhat different circumstances.
This move failed, and in 1958 the governments of
Tunisia and Morocco, and the Provisional Government
of the Algerian Republic proclaimed a confederal structure, which was not seriously implemented because of
the continuing French rule over Algeria. This was a
clear case of utilizing unity as a weapon in the fight
for independence.

The vagaries of the decolonization process, insofar as
they have affected the possibilities of African unity,
have not been entirely fortuitous. Colonial governments were not entirely indifferent to these questions.
On the contrary, it can be argued that France was systematically, although not outspokenly, hostile, the British to a limited degree favorable, and the Belgians
veered sharply between extremes.

Between 1956 and 1960, as French black African
territories went from colonial status to autonomy to
independence, the French seldom threw their support
to elements favorable to larger political unities. The
reason was very simple. Those who most strongly advocated unity were also those who most strongly pushed
the advances toward independence. French repudiation
of the goal of independence led to deep suspicion of the
goal of unity. This was true of their attitude toward
the moves made in this period to establish strong federal executives in French West Africa and French
Equatorial Africa. The same was true of their attitude
toward the reunification of both Togo and Cameroun
with their British trust counterparts. It was true, as
well, of their view of the pan-Somali movement in
French Somaliland. And of course the French would
never sympathize with moves for North African unity
because these moves were predicated on the assumption
of Algerian independence from France.

The British position was less clear-cut. In the early colonial era, they too sought to divide and conquer. But once they came to terms with the nationalist movement in a particular area, they looked with favor on achieving larger unities, chiefly on the grounds that larger entities showed more potential for stability and economic development. We have already mentioned the case of British Somaliland. There, having long opposed pan-Somali tendencies, the British surprised everyone, including the Somalis, by timing British Somaliland's independence to coincide with that of Somalia. In Nigeria, the British bore much responsibility for the rise of regionalism. But once having decided to go forward to independence, the British, between 1956 and 1960, were one of the important forces working toward the establishment of the strongest possible federal state for an independent Nigeria. In the settler territories of East and Central Africa, the Colonial Office was historically a stalwart supporter of moves toward federation, imposing its point of view on the Africans and to some extent even on the settlers. Nevertheless, by 1960 British support had somewhat abated as a result of the persistent African opposition. At this stage, having once again decided to go forward to independence (with universal suffrage), the British sought means of preserving the federal link (tainted by its association with white-settler domination) between the future independent African states. The work of the Monckton Commission in Central Africa and the Raisman Commission in East Africa are illustrations.

The factor that has made for the greatest difference between the British and the French attitudes toward larger unities in Africa has been the British willingness to acknowledge the legitimacy of the goal of independence. This has enabled the British, during the transition period, to look ahead to the postindependence period and plan their policy accordingly. They have thus always been able to take a more relaxed view of African unity than the French.

The Belgian policy has been quite different from both the French and the British. The Belgians had always ruled the Congo as a unitary state with some administrative decentralization. When they decided to grant the Congo its independence, they were eager to retain this unitary character. They feared that separatist movements would destroy the strong economy of the Congo in which they intended to remain involved.* Shortly after independence, when it appeared that Belgium's continuing political and economic relationship with the Congo was threatened by the strong supporters of the unitary state, the Belgian government veered to a strong support of separatist, indeed secessionist, elements.

The policies of the colonial powers in relation to larger African unities can be seen to reflect their views of their own interests. That Britain, France and Belgium analyzed these interests differently does not detract from the reality of this motivation. Even insofar as colonial powers were favorable to unity, it was a unity within the family, so to speak. When it came to moves for pan-African unity that cut across the traditional colonial divisions, even the more sanguine British hesitated occasionally. Yet, of course, African unity will have real meaning only in the degree to which the new entities will cut across divisions of European language and demarcations of European colonial spheres.

What concrete achievements can be pointed to as evidence of the reality of pan-African aspirations? There were, first of all, the Conferences of Independent African States, in Accra in 1958, in Addis Ababa in 1960. These were among the several successors to the Pan-

* However, during this period, 1959–60, the *French* government, characteristically, gave tacit encouragement to the Bakongo separatists led by Joseph Kasavubu.

African Congresses. Up to now these assemblies have been largely resolution-passing bodies, but they have been able to secure the adherence of all the independent states.* The one permanent structure to grow out of these Conferences was the African bloc at the United Nations which, by regular meetings of the permanent representatives of the African states, forged an impressive unity between 1958 and 1960. With the admission of sixteen more African nations in the 1960 session of the United Nations and the divisive explosion of the Congo, this unity at least temporarily disappeared.

Parallel with these Conferences of Independent African States have been the meetings of the All-African People's Conferences (AAPC), another of the successors to the Pan-African Congresses.† The AAPC groups include nationalist political parties and trade-union federations of both independent and not-yet-independent African countries. Hitherto the major concern of the AAPC has been the liberation of the remaining colonial Africa. The first meeting was held in Accra in 1958, followed by one in Tunis in 1959, and a third in Cairo in 1961. The AAPC has set up a continuing machinery, a secretariat whose headquarters is Accra. The first secretary general was George Padmore, Trinidadian and close collaborator of Nkrumah, with whom he was joint secretary of the 1945 Manchester Pan-African Congress. When Padmore died in 1959, he was succeeded by Abdoulaye Diallo, Guinea's resident minister in Ghana and former trade-union leader in French West Africa.

It is important to note the close links, through personnel and ideology, between the Conferences of Independent African States and the All-African People's

* Except the Union of South Africa, which was actually invited to the 1958 Accra Conference but refused to come because the colonial powers were not invited also.

† The third major successor, the Congresses of Black Men of Culture. we shall discuss in Chapter VII.

Conferences. The latter have been the nongovernmental
parallel to the intergovernmental body,* and have had
a certain flexibility of maneuver, structure, and even
language from which the exigencies of government
protocol restrain the former. It is also important to
note that both these structures have joined together
black sub-Saharan Africa and Arab North Africa. This
has been not peripheral but central to the conception.
Indeed, thus far, these structures have been better at
bringing together black and Arab Africa than at bringing together French-speaking and English-speaking Africa. The structures thus far have not been able to involve some of the significant groups in French-speaking
black Africa, despite the fact that the North African
participants are largely French-speaking. This was because, as we explained earlier, some of the French
Africans have resisted greater African unity.

Many of the forces behind the AAPC have attempted to create an All-African Trade Union Federation (AATUF) as a concrete method of furthering
African unity. Here there has been an added complication: Some African trade unions today are members of
the International Confederation of Free Trade Unions
(ICFTU), a non-Communist body.† One of the force
behind AATUF has been the Union Générale de
Travailleurs de l'Afrique Noire (UGTAN), an interterritorial group whose base was in former French West
Africa.‡ UGTAN achieved internal unity in 1957 by

* The same double structure of intergovernment meetings on
the one hand and interparty, inter-trade-union and interstudent
organization meetings on the other hand has been used on a
smaller geographic scale in North Africa.

† A few less important unions belong to the International
Federation of Christian Trade Unions; also a very few belong to
the Communist-dominated World Federation of Trade Unions.
Finally, there are a large number affiliated with none of these
internationals.

‡ The headquarters were in Conakry, Guinea, and the president of UGTAN was Sékou Touré, President of the Republic of
Guinea, who started his political career as a trade-union leader

getting all the constituent members to break ties with internationals—"positive neutrality" on the trade-union scene. UGTAN leaders and others have thought that such international nonaffiliation should be the basis of the projected AATUF. Some trade unions affiliated with the ICFTU, notably those of Tunisia and Kenya, have argued that they do not wish to cut their ties with the ICFTU. This quarrel has made the realization of AATUF difficult. But here again it should be noted that all the preparatory meetings for AATUF have included both North and sub-Saharan Africans, both French-speaking and English-speaking black Africans, and the divisions over international affiliations have crosscut the geographical and language differences. Similar efforts in the field of youth and students' groups have been even more tentative.

On the intergovernmental level, the chances for unity, as we have seen, were affected by the decolonization process. We have mentioned the real, if partial, success of the pan-Somali movement, as well as the more limited results of efforts to create a unified North Africa. There has also been the reunification of Cameroun with the southern half of the British Cameroons, as well as the earlier federation of Eritrea with Ethiopia.

In French black Africa, we have shown, decolonization worked against unity. This was particularly evident in the attempt to create a federation of French West Africa. Though originally there were eight territories, an attempt to create a structure called the Federation of Mali could rally only four, of which two failed to ratify the constitution, and the remaining two, after a year and a half of coexistence, broke apart in August 1960. One move intended to counter the Federation of Mali was the Conseil de l'Entente, a loose confederation of sovereign states. The Conseil de l'Entente was as much a move designed to prevent unity (of the federal Mali variety) as one to promote unity. Another attempt in former French Equatorial

Africa to found a federal Union des Républiques d'Afrique Centrale (URAC)—similar in conception to Mali —foundered before it was ever ratified. As for plans to establish unities that transcended colonial spheres, the proposal of the Abbé Boganda for a United States of Latin Africa (to group Cameroun, Congo, Angola and the four states of former French Equatorial Africa) and the plans of the Senegalese for Senegambia (to incorporate the tiny British colony of the Gambia into Senegal or, at one point, into the Federation of Mali) never got beyond the talking stage.

On the other hand, out of the destruction of French West African unity caused by the process of decolonization came the construction of one political unity that does transcend colonial language barriers, the Ghana-Guinea Union in 1959.* Ghana and Guinea do not have contiguous frontiers, and the Union has no structure beyond the fact that the two countries exchange not ambassadors but resident ministers, who have the right to attend the cabinet meetings of the partner. The Union has neither common institutions, common language, nor common currency. And yet it would be rash to discount it. For the Union has brought together two dynamic countries which, despite many common attitudes, had almost no contact until the very time of the Union. The Union may be thought to be nothing but a very strong alliance, which is all it amounts to in terms of structure. But its significance lies in the fact that it symbolizes the possibility of transcending the "language barrier" and, by this very fact alone, is a force of attraction for pan-Africanists throughout Africa.

Ghana and Guinea both separately and together are major pressures toward African unity. Their force lies in their internal strength and dynamism, their vigorous positions on international affairs, their neutralism, their constant efforts to promote liberation in colonial

* To which the *Republic* of Mali adhered in 1960, making it the Union of African States.

territories and to support, financially and otherwise,
pan-Africanist elements. The North Africans represent
another such pressure, not always a united one. Presenting an image of themselves as Africans first, Arabs
second, they are working very hard to see that African
unity includes them, although they may conceive of
this unity as a coalition of regional frameworks (such
as North Africa, West Africa, East and Central Africa,
etc.).

The United Arab Republic (UAR) is often credited
with being a major force in pan-Africanism. Actually,
despite money expended both in propaganda and in
assistance to various nationalist movements in their
anticolonial struggles, and despite the fact that at
various points some nationalist leaders (for example
those of Algeria, Cameroun, Uganda) have had bureaus
in Cairo, the UAR has played only a minor role. The
reason is that their image of themselves, as well as
that which other Africans have of them, is of a country
primarily interested in Arab unity and only secondarily
concerned with all-African unity.

It is more significant to ask what are the present and
future roles of Nigeria and the Ivory Coast. Nigeria,
Africa's largest country in population, enjoys the prestige and power of its size and the fact that in itself it
represents an achievement in terms of African unity.
Thus far, the need to maintain the balance of internal
unity has kept it from playing the downstage role of
Ghana in the pan-African movement. However, the
very fact that Nigeria considers Ghana's role an exaggerated one may push her to advocate pan-African
doctrines even more strongly. The Ivory Coast, by
contrast, has shown itself cool to larger unities which
would impinge on her own autonomy and development.
Unable to fight pan-Africanist forces alone, the Ivory
Coast has taken the lead in creating the Entente,
as well as a coöperative arrangement of a larger group

of French-speaking states (Abidjan, Brazzaville, and Yaoundé Conferences of 1960–61).

The Congo crisis temporarily divided most of the half of Africa which was independent in 1960 into two camps: the strong pan-Africanists who attended the Casablanca Conference, and the advocates of a milder form of unity who attended the Brazzaville Conference. This crystallization into separate units is only momentary, however. As East, Central and South Africa attain independent governments based on universal suffrage, the crosscutting alliances should begin to make the realization of African unity a reality.

It is clear from this discussion that not all Africans and not all African states are equally pan-African in their enthusiasm. What should be noted is that there is some correlation (not a perfect one) in each African state between those elements who are modernizing and centralizing and those who are oriented to pan-Africanism. The strength of the pan-African drive can be attributed precisely to the fact that it is the weapon of the modernizers—those throughout Africa who are most radical in their nationalism, most vigorous in their demands for equality, most conscious of the primacy of political solutions to the problems of Africa. Pan-Africanism may one day be divorced from modernization in Africa. It is not so today. To the extent, then, that pan-Africanism fails, modernization too is set back.

:VII:

CULTURAL REVIVAL

In the colonial era, whether the system of administration was direct or indirect, whether assimilation was or was not a specifically developed policy in the educational and judicial spheres, the Europeans in Africa—administrators or traders, missionaries or educators—shared one basic assumption: the superiority of Western cultural values to those they found in African countries. Moreover, they usually assumed that they had, in one form or another, what the French liked to call a "civilizing mission," which always meant a Westernizing mission and quite often meant a Christianizing mission. This was no passing mood. It was the fundamental ideological justification of the whole colonial enterprise. And it was a justification which Europeans sought to have the African educated elite accept.

To some degree, this policy of cultural denigration of African society was successful. The African intellectuals did at first reject their own culture—not only its religion and its technology, but its dress and its music, and most important, its link with the past. These intellectuals very largely accepted the notion that Africa had no history, that the future lay in adopting a Western style of life.

We have seen how the nationalist movement, for various reasons, ultimately rejected the alternative of assimilation as a means of achieving political equality and went on to demand political independence. In the political sphere, the choice, once clarified, was a simple one. Either total assimilation or total separation would assure equality. Nothing in between would do. But in cultural questions, the problem was the opposite, how both to assimilate and preserve, how both to be universal and to be oneself, how to modernize without being Western.

For its own organizational purposes, the nationalist movement began to find much virtue in cultural revival. In seeking to turn a protonationalist movement that was limited to an educated urban group into a mass nationalist movement that could appeal to peasant masses who were still strongly traditional in outlook, nationalist leaders began to rediscover and praise the heroes of ancient Africa once more. They would choose most particularly the heroes who had resisted the colonial powers, especially those whose empires had been expanding at the moment of European contact. Thus the West African Mandingo chief Samory and the Zulu king Chaka, the Mad Mullah of Somalia and Abd-el-Kader of Algeria, all treated in colonial textbooks as barbarians, as cruel warriors whose conquest or defeat was the beginning of progress, came to be seen once again as noble victims of colonial rapacity. An objective analysis of their role is not to the point. The point is that the nationalist movement began to reject the colonial interpretation of recent events. Many nationalist leaders sought to trace their own lines of descent (some spurious) from these earlier kings and heroes. Jomo Kenyatta, working under the British anthropologist Malinowski in the 1930's, shocked the colonial world with his ethnographic survey of the Kikuyu, *Facing Mount Kenya*, by making it an open defense of many Kikuyu customs, including female circumcision. He wrote: "The missionaries who attack the *irua* of girls are more to be pitied than condemned, for most of their information is derived from Gikuyu converts who have been taught by these same Christians to regard the custom of female circumcision as something savage and barbaric, worthy only of heathens who live in perpetual sin under the influence of the Devil." Up to that time, no African intellectual had dared openly to question the illegitimacy of such traditional practices.

Yet a nationalist movement must be cautious. Seeking to find themes that will draw it mass support, seeking the enlistment of traditional attitudes and grievances on behalf of a modern cause, the nationalist movement risks losing more than it gains—and on two fronts. At home, as we have seen, the traditional rulers were quite often closely bound up with the colonial administration. Traditional themes could be used against, as much as in favor of, uprooted urban intellectuals. Furthermore, nationalists had to consider international public opinion, which played such an important role in the timing and ease of transition. At the critical moment of the "time of troubles," and still more so during the dyarchy, the nationalist movement hesitated to risk alienating the outside world. Compare the Mau Mau rebellion with the Algerian rebellion. Mau Mau repelled large segments of British and world opinion. Even Kenyan nationalist leaders tried to remain unassociated with it (at least at the time). This was one reason—of course not the only one—why Mau Mau could be crushed. The Algerians, even when they used means of violence which met with reprobation in the outside world, did so in a Western tradition to which they pointed as justification. Presenting a resolutely modernist image, and toning down terrorist tactics under international pressure, the Algerians were able to use international sympathy as a major tool in their struggle.

The colonial situation, then, placed many limitations on cultural revival, both by the direct pressure of the

administration and the indirect one of international
opinion. Independence would lift these restraints. Indeed, the demands of national integration would press
directly for more cultural revival, which in turn would
create new dilemmas for the new states. But before we
consider these dilemmas, let us see what are the forms
and expressions of African cultural revival: in the writing of history, in philosophy and religion, in linguistic
matters, in literature and the arts, and even in political
and economic theory.

The primary fact to note about the revival of African
history is the uphill battle that had to be fought to
demonstrate the very existence of the thing to be studied. A cardinal premise of colonial rule had been that
"Africa has no history." In the schools of the colonial
era, the African history that was taught was the history
of the colonial era. French African schoolchildren used
a notorious textbook that began "Our ancestors the
Gauls." Neither European nor any other universities
had chairs for African history or men specializing in
African history. A certain historical past was accredited
at most to North Africa, but that area was treated as
part of the Mediterranean world, and the importance
of the Arab part of its history quite often minimized.
As for black Africa, since it was believed there were
no written records and since Africans were thought
incapable of higher cultural achievement, it was considered inconceivable to apply the term history to the
story of unchanging savage cultures.

But as we have seen in Chapter I, the history of
Africa shows diversity and change, development and
progress, like the histories of other continents. And
since our knowledge of this history, though greatly
enlarged in very recent years, has been acquired grad-
ually over at least a century, how was it that Europeans
maintained the image of an Africa without history?
They did so by systematically refusing to believe that
the archaeological finds, the works of art uncovered,

the travelers' tales of ancient empires were the products of a black civilization. Indeed, a European in 1895
doubted the African origin of some ruins in Rhodesia:
"It is a well-accepted fact that the negroid brain never
could be capable of taking the initiative in work of such
intricate nature."

All sorts of people—the "whiter" the better—got
credit for these works. There were, as we have seen,
the ubiquitous Hamites who seemed to be everywhere
and were at least not Bantus. There were "Hittites"
and "Phoenicians," Arabs in East Africa, Jews and
Berbers in West Africa, and even the ancient Greeks or
the Portuguese later on. Not all of this was fiction,
but much of it was. It has been proved, for example,
that ancient Greek ships were technically incapable of
reaching West Africa, given their construction and the
tides. In any case, serious scholarly proof was seldom
attempted. On the contrary, many persons seemed to
reach out deliberately for improbable explanations of
obvious situations so as to maintain the myths in
which they so profoundly believed. Even some anthropologists, who could have been expected to be
more sympathetic to the reality of African achievement,
tended rather to search for primitive purity—which
seemed by implication to deny any higher achievement.

Since the Second World War, there has been a new
way of looking at African history. First there were a
number of European, American and Soviet scholars
(archaeologists, historians, anthropologists, art historians, even ethnobotanists) who began to make important new discoveries that helped to create an understandable pattern of the migratory movements and of
the rise and fall of African empires. But it was the
emergence of African scholarship about Africa that did
most to create a significant change in atmosphere. The
way was prepared by an older generation of amateur
African scholars—ministers, schoolmasters, lawyers—
whose research, if not always of the highest quality,

was inspired by a feeling that the themes they were treating were important and had been neglected. Their work has been taken up now by African historians, sociologists and anthropologists of full professional status, especially those in West Africa—men like Nigeria's K. O. Dike and S. O. Biobaku, Ghana's K. A. Busia and Nana Nketsia, Senegal's Cheikh Anta Diop and Ly Abdoulaye, and Joseph Ki Zerbo of Upper Volta.

The revival of history was important for the anti-colonial revolution, not only to create a justification for nationalism in terms of the past but to destroy the myth of European virtue that enchained so many of the educated group. It began to break down the effectiveness of the myth of white superiority in the colony, even among the European colonials, and in the metropolitan country. Thus it built up African confidence as it lessened European. After independence the rewriting of history became central to the evolution of the new nation.

We have already remarked that one of the problems of national integration is that most African nations have only a short past as nationalities, and that this means that the concept of loyalty to the nation has no roots in tradition. Conscious efforts have been made by African governments to review educational curricula at all levels in order to reorient the history that is taught. Many countries have built museums before libraries. Historical journals have been started for the educated elite, and children's books are being written on African historical themes.

It is for the intellectual particularly that this re-awakening historical sense seems to be important. He who was most conscious of being cut off from his cultural heritage now turns to it with a vengeance and a fascination. His concern is not merely the practical one of discovering themes which will somehow create a national consciousness among the peasantry. It is the

classic concern of the intellectual who finds himself
somehow out of the mainstream of his society's attitudes and ways of life, and seeks a way of personal re-
integration into the community. Precisely insofar as the
intellectuals have found some difficulty in achieving
political power in the new African nations, precisely
insofar as they have been uncomfortable in the shadow
of a heroic leader, they have turned to their specialty—
cultural nationalism, the interweaving of new and old
myths.

It is interesting to see what subjects they have concentrated on. One, obviously, is the period of colonial
conquest. There have been works to underline the
economic interests involved in colonial "pacification,"
the profits extracted by cruelty. Or there have been
works trying to demonstrate that African empires such
as the Ashanti or Zulu were at important points of
consolidation and expansion when forcibly stopped and
partially destroyed by European forces; that is, that
important African achievements went unrealized because of colonial penetration. This kind of historical
focus is understandable and will continue for a long
time. The documents are reasonably ample and the
material scarcely has been touched. Aspects of history
that usually have been avoided thus far are the more
recent colonial period and the nationalist movements.
The material in these fields is perhaps *too* recent. In
any case, the authors are often too involved in this
very history, and find the subjects too delicate. There
are some exceptions, like *The Sudan Question*, by Mekki
Abbas. And there are, of course, the growing number
of autobiographies by leading African politicians that
are, to some extent, short histories of the nationalist
movements of their countries (for example, the autobiographies of Bourguiba, Nkrumah, Awolowo).

The historical problem that has evoked the greatest
interest in Africa is one which is much less often the
focus of Western European history. This is the question

of origins, the problem of looking into the far past and trying to see where Africans as a whole, or a given African people, originated. In Chapter I we reviewed some of the facts known at the present time. What we emphasize here is the nature of the interest and the reasons for it.

On analysis, it is not so surprising to find that Africans place great emphasis on this question of origins. First of all, to discuss origins, one has to turn to a remote past, shrouded in mystery because of lack of documents. The very remoteness in time of the subject matter emphasizes the historical existence of the group under study, their presence in the world *over a long period of time*. Second, as one pushes back in time, the disparity in technology between a given African society and any other society is less than at present; indeed, the comparison may well be to the advantage of the African society. Third, it may be possible to demonstrate not merely the nonsuperiority of Western civilization but, conversely, the superiority of African civilization, if one pushes the analysis sufficiently far back.

So far much of this writing on origins has been about West African peoples, perhaps because nationalism had an earlier start there. In East, Central and South Africa, which are faced with claims of white settlers to the rights of permanent inhabitants, Africans emphasize how long they have been in the area rather than where they came from at some earlier period. It may be that once independent African states exist in this area, they too may begin to explore their origins.

In West Africa, two peoples particularly have been the focus of historical interest: the Akan and the Yoruba. The Akan peoples include most of the major tribes of the southern half of the Gold Coast. In 1926 the Rev. W. T. Balmer suggested that these peoples derived from the inhabitants of the ancient empire of Ghana. He argued that after the destruction of the empire these people migrated southeast a thousand miles to their present habitat. The claim was based partly on tribal legends which indicated such a migration. The Rev. Mr. Balmer's idea might have lapsed into obscurity had it not been picked up, amplified and reinvigorated after World War II by Gold Coast nationalist politicians, particularly Dr. J. B. Danquah. This claim of descent became so important a theme of Gold Coast politics that it overrode all factional differences, and Ghana was selected in 1957 as the name of the newly independent nation. Scholars are still arguing over the validity of the claim, but the name of Ghana will remain.* As for the Yorubas, the first suggestion that they migrated from Egypt, again partly based on tribal legends, was made in the nineteenth century by an African Anglican bishop. In this case, too, the claim was picked up and emphasized in the post-World War II period, and the Nigerian Western Regional government invested special funds in furthering the study. The Yoruba claim has had a strong Christian bias, and there has been some attempt to show parallels between Yoruba customs and those of the ancient Hebrews.

Perhaps the most ambitious attempt to reconstruct African history has been the numerous writings of Cheikh Anta Diop. Diop has a theory that there is a basic global division of peoples into two kinds: the Southerners (or Negro-Africans), and the Aryans (a category covering all Caucasians, including Semites, Mongoloids and American Indians). Each grouping has a cultural outlook based on response to climate, the difference between them being that the Aryans have had a harsher climate.

The Aryans have developed patriarchal systems characterized by the suppression of women and a propensity

* Another ancient empire, Mali, gave its name to a new nation, formerly the French Sudan, but in this case Mali was presumed to have occupied somewhat the same territory.

for war. Also associated with such societies are materialist religion, sin and guilt, xenophobia, the tragic drama, the city-state, individualism and pessimism. Southerners, on the other hand, are matriarchal. The women are free and the people peaceful; there is a Dionysian approach to life, religious idealism and no concept of sin. With a matriarchal society come xenophilia, the tale as the literary form, the territorial state, social collectivism, and optimism.

According to Diop's theory, the ancient Egyptians, who were Negroes, are the ancestors of the Southerners. This bold hypothesis, which is not presented without supporting data, has the interesting effect of inverting Western cultural assumptions.* For, Diop argues, if the ancient Egyptians were Negroes, then European civilization is but a derivation of African achievement. He writes: "It is impossible to insist on everything the world—in particular, the Hellenic world—owes the Egyptian world. The Greeks did nothing but take up and sometimes, to a degree, develop Egyptian inventions, all the while despoiling them, because of their materialist tendencies, of the idealistic religious shell which surrounded them." Thus, even Western technology is traced to its Egyptian (Negro) origins.

Not all African scholarship is this sweeping in its claims. But another aspect of African culture has received special attention in recent years: its philosophy and religion. Perhaps the greatest contribution in these fields has been made by a non-African Catholic priest, Father Tempels. Father Tempels, in his book *The Bantu Philosophy*, based on long research through African informants, analyzed the cosmological ideas of the Bantu people. He discovered them to be highly complex, and fundamentally monogamous in spirit. He discovered that one could talk of a Bantu ontology, a

* The hypothesis is not original with Diop. Other scholars, such as W. E. B. Du Bois, had earlier presented the argument that the ancient Egyptians were Negroes.

Bantu psychology, a Bantu ethic, and concluded that these "discoveries" made it necessary to revise basic European attitudes toward the African. Father Tempels ended his book by offering an apology for those Europeans who had previously disdained African thought. The book was written in 1944–45 and contributed to the new spirit of the postwar period.

Similar work by the French anthropologist Marcel Griaule among the Dogon of the western Sudan further undermined assumptions of African primitivity. In this same region the works of an African sage of this century, Tierno Bokar, have been presented to the intellectual public by his disciple, Amadou Ba Hampaté, who was named the first director of the research institute of the Republic of Mali. African Catholic priests (and some Protestants) have tried to review Christian rituals and their relation to African customs and have sought new syntheses that would allow the universal principles of Christianity to take on a specifically African form. African philosophy and theology, drawing upon the traditions known to African soil, have become living and creative disciplines.

This revival of history and philosophy has been part of a wider movement known as negritude, the earliest spokesmen of which were poets. Two very significant facts should be noted about negritude. First, the word is French and for a long time the movement has been dominated by the French-speaking African world, perhaps because of their greater revolt against previous assimilationist tendencies. Second, the word was invented not by an African but by a West Indian Negro, Aimé Césaire of Martinique, and then picked up by Léopold Senghor, a poet who is now the President of Senegal.

Organizationally, the proponents of negritude in 1947 founded a magazine, *Présence Africaine*, edited by a Senegalese, Alioune Diop, and published in Paris.*

* An English edition was started in 1958.

The intellectual ferment that grew out of this magazine
led its participants to convene the first World Congress
of Black Men of Culture in Paris in 1956, and another
in Rome in 1959. The lines of admission to these Congresses have not been absolutely clear. Congresses of
the Negro world, they have included inhabitants of
black Africa and Negroes from the United States, the
Caribbean, and Brazil. However, they also have included Malagasies, who are of Malaysian stock, but
whose island, Madagascar, is considered part of the
African continent and whose present political history
has been closely tied to that of black Africa. And
North African (Arab) intellectuals have tried to maintain a special relationship with these Congresses. The
first Congress created an international African Society
of Culture, whose explicit model was the European
Society of Culture.

The definition of negritude, and the determination of
the scope of "African culture," has not been a simple
matter; indeed it has been the central point of debate
among these intellectuals. There have been two main
trends within this movement. One point of view has
been that negritude is a matter of form, of some innate
emotional quality of the Negro soul which binds Negroes the world over. Senghor has been a leading exponent of this point of view, characterizing the Negro in
terms of intuitiveness and sensitivity, qualities thought
to be derived from the Negro's tropical agricultural
existence but now hereditary. He has said: "That
which constitutes the Negritude of a poem is less the
theme than the style, the emotional fervor which gives
life to the words, which converts the words into speech."
Cheikh Anta Diop's theories make a similar assumption
of some special quality in African culture. This is why
both these men have preferred to speak of Negro-
African rather than of African culture.

Another point of view is that negritude is a quality of
revolt which derives from the political and cultural

oppression the Negro has known. Jean-Paul Sartre
adopted this viewpoint in his famous essay, "Black
Orpheus," in which he described contemporary Negro
literature as the only revolutionary literature in the
contemporary world. This is also the viewpoint of
Jacques Rabemananjara, Malagasy poet, politician,
and major contributor to *Présence Africaine*, who has
said: "Now who forges these arms of salvation? It is
not the Negro as a Negro; it is the Negro as one frustrated, it is the Negro as one humiliated in the depths
of his soul, it is the Negro as one mutilated in his
dignity as a human being. . . . I do not know further
how belonging to Negritude has ever dictated to its
poets an esthetic attitude." *

Clearly the second point of view is more compatible
with a pan-African political unity that would include
North Africa than the former approach. Clearly, too,
it is more in line with the dominant trends of Western
thought. The division between these two outlooks,
however, is by no means sharp; negritude, African cultural nationalism, is still garnering its forces and feeling
its way. But this division, which arose out of the ambi-
guities of the movement for African independence
(movement against racism, movement against colonialism, movement for supranational unity), may mean
that what we have called the third legatee of the Pan-
African Congresses may someday move away from the
other two, more directly political, legatees (the Conferences of Independent African States and the All-
African People's Conferences). For the moment, this
is not so.

These theoretical differences about the nature of
negritude have not been without their immediate implications, even in what might seem so remote a field
as political and economic theory. For a long time Afri-

* The South African author Ezekiel Mphalehle represents a
third group, which is deeply suspicious of possible "racist" implications of negritude.

can nationalism has had as one of its subthemes the establishment in the new nations of an "African socialism." The adjective "African" is significant, for it has been argued that, in the process of technological advance and economic development, there is no reason to adopt Western economic structures, either capitalist or state socialist, when the traditional African communal ownership of land offers the base for a coöperative socialist economy with a peculiarly African stamp. This emphasis on the coöperative in the economic structure, made most explicit by Mamadou Dia, economist and Prime Minister of Senegal, has been matched in the field of political structure by the contention of Guinea's Sékou Touré that Africa's traditional political structure—what he calls "communocracy"—can be the basis of a peculiarly African form of democracy. Julius Nyerere of Tanganyika, arguing the same point, has called the African "communitary" in his thinking. In these theories of Dia, Touré and Nyerere can be found a middle road between those who see an almost physiological uniqueness about African culture and those who view it purely in universal terms. These economic and social theories have been arguments for universal values within the forms of traditional African institutions, for being modern without being Western.

The cultural revival of Africa presents no simple, clear pattern. Revival always implies a selection of the past, a selection that is made not only in terms of the exigencies of the present but of the plans for the future. We revive the past, but which past? Biobaku writes of the origin of the Yoruba and Cheikh Anta Diop of the origin of the Negro-African, while Algerians speak of "we Africans." Each may have a different image of Africa; certainly each enterprise, each locution will have a definite bearing on the future structure of African society.

If cultural revival has caused much pain, it is in part because it both abets and hurts the process of modernization. Adopting the techniques of another culture, when that culture has been dominant politically until only recently, is a very hard thing for a people to accept. The psychological stance is one of weakness, of lack of self-confidence. The danger is that if one feels weak, one finds any change threatening and therefore rejects all change. Mau Mau was a momentary instance of this attitude. The reassertion of the values of African culture, the creation of an African cultural unity, can instill a sense of security in Africa such that it will be able to adopt technological changes from outside Africa, principally the Western world, without fear that these adoptions will destroy the African character, the "African personality," of the independent nations.

But the revival of tradition means also the strengthening of the traditional elite. The two cannot be separated entirely. Having fought the traditional elite in the colonial era, the modernizing intellectual elite is in no mood to cede power after independence. Yet to build the unity of a nation, to give it the psychological strength to be modern, the modernizing elite must in part reassert tradition and reinforce some traditional institutions. In this new alliance, whereby the traditional elite is absorbed into the party structures, the question of the future remains: who will control whom? This is particularly the question at the village level. What seem like monolithic parties from the outside are often the scenes of subtle, or not so subtle, struggles inside, between those forces who stand against change and those who stand for modernization. Both present themselves as the exponents of an African way. But the party structure is an uneasy meeting ground, and the future developments remain uncertain.

:VIII:

AFRICA

AND THE WORLD

Having emerged from colonial rule, Africa is determined to be subject to no one but itself. And Africa is determined somehow to be distinctively different, distinctively African. The depth of its sensitivity to outside control, the suspicion of outside links, should not be misinterpreted, however. It is not a rejection of the world. It is an embracement of it. For African nationalists held, as one of their cardinal criticisms of colonial rule, that it maintained Africans in a cocoon, that the colonial administration hindered contacts with, even knowledge about, areas and peoples outside the particular network. Independence was accompanied by a strong desire to taste the forbidden fruit, to visit and enter into relations with all those parts of the world somehow previously withheld from Africans. Yet, paradoxically, Africans feel they can guarantee this continued contact with the whole world best by emphasizing the autonomy, even the apartness, of Africa. They see pan-Africanism not as the creation of a supernationalism but as a means of contributing to the spirit and reality of world coöperation.

The coöperation of Africa with the rest of the world

takes many forms. The form that is still dominant in most cases, despite decolonization, is the link with the former metropolitan power. In some cases, this is a strong link, formed by institutions and affective ties. In others, it is a reluctant link, made necessary by economy and language. And even where there has been a sharp and bitter break, as in Guinea or the Congo, there continue to be important ties.

These links can take the form of formal structures: the Commonwealth of Nations, or the "renovated" Community, for example. Ghana, Nigeria, Sierra Leone are in the Commonwealth; Senegal, Gabon, Madagascar are in the Community. But the Sudan, a former British colony,* is not a Commonwealth member. Tunisia, Mali, the Ivory Coast, Togo, among others, are not in the Community. Libya and Somalia are not politically linked to Italy, nor the Congo to Belgium. The peculiarities of the political evolution of each colony, particularly during the period of decolonization, explain which remain in these structures and which do not.

Participation in these structures involves meetings of chiefs of governments or their ministers on an irregular basis, normally some reciprocal privileges for citizens (sometimes the right to dual citizenship), sometimes juridical structures. To symbolize the special relationship, Commonwealth states recognize the Queen of England as the "head of the Commonwealth," and Community states the President of France as "head of the Community.' These states exchange not ambassadors but "high commissioners" for the Commonwealth, and "high representatives" for the Community.† The details of the relationship are worked out separately for any given pair, for these structures have

* Technically speaking, it was an Anglo-Egyptian Condominium. But during much of this time, Egypt was under British rule.

† Similarly, Ghana, Guinea, and Mali, because of their union, exchange not ambassadors but resident ministers.

turned out to be highly pragmatic legal entities. The ties between these structures are not very different from the ties of treaty and diplomatic recognition that African states which have chosen full independence maintain with the former colonial power. There is a wide spectrum of possibilities for interweaving the two countries, by means of which former colonial powers retain certain privileges in return for making certain concessions, often economic.

The link that may last the longest, and is perhaps the most real today, is that of language and, to a lesser extent, of culture. For all African independent states have retained their colonial language as the language of the elite. Even where Arabic has been reintroduced in North Africa, these states have retained the colonial language as either an official or second language (French in Morocco and Tunisia, English in Egypt and the Sudan, Italian in Libya). Even the primary schools in many African independent states utilize the colonial language, certainly the secondary schools and the universities. With the enormous expansion of educational institutions after independence, and the equally great shortage of teachers, the new African nations have had to rely heavily on recruiting teachers from the former colonial powers. Thus, even when relations were most exacerbated between France and Morocco, Tunisia, or Guinea, a special diplomatic effort was always made on both sides to keep the flow of teachers open.

A similar flow in the reverse direction, the flow of African students to the universities of the former colonial power, is also kept open. In most cases the majority of students from a given African nation studying abroad —in almost all cases at least the plurality—are in the metropolitan universities. Given the paucity of African institutions of higher learning, this means that at the present time a large percentage of all university graduates studied in the former colonial country, and that a smaller but still substantial part of the annual output of university graduates continue to have studied there. This cannot help but mean a continuing cultural link with the former colonial power.

The continuing cultural influence of the former metropole is a hard thing to measure. We have already outlined in Chapter IV the legacies of the different colonial administrations. Despite the reaction against these European cultural influences, despite African cultural revival and pan-Africanism, the stamp of the colonial cultural heritage is still strong and is perpetuated among the intellectuals by the continuing flow of students to metropolitan universities. It is perpetuated too by the channels of communication. Politicians and intellectuals in former French areas still tend to read *Le Monde*, *L'Express*, *France-Observateur;* and in former British areas, they read *The Times*, the *Guardian*, the *New Statesman and Nation*, and *The Economist*. This is especially true because there are almost no African papers or journals in the independent states that give reasonable coverage of international happenings.* Because of the use of these European channels of information, a Dahomean today may still be more aware of the nuances of politics in Vietnam—the link of the old French Empire—than of those of his neighbor Nigeria. This situation may not last. If the political impulses of pan-Africanism are reinforced by newspapers and cultural exchanges that cross language barriers—which is happening increasingly—then the corresponding cultural ties among African states should increase and those with the former colonial powers should weaken.

The economic links that bind former colonies to Europe are presently even more important than the cultural links, although they may turn out to be less enduring. In a majority of cases, African independent nations remain in either the sterling or the franc monetary zones. They are, however, in the process of developing their own national banks, and there are a

* *Afrique-Action*, published in Tunis since 1960, is an exception.

variety of special arrangements with the former colonial powers concerning the control of currency transactions.

There are also continuing reciprocal customs concessions. Furthermore, for the former colonies of France, Belgium and Italy, there is the possibility of remaining within the orbit of the European Economic Community, which thus gives them certain trade advantages over their African neighbors.* Perhaps most fundamentally of all, trade and investment channels still remain largely in the old colonial rut. There are few African independent states, the majority, or at least plurality, of whose exports and imports are not with the former colonial power. The strength of established business connections, the difficulties and expense of reconversion of all kinds of machinery and durable goods help to maintain this pattern. The relationship between colonial power and independent state is also reinforced by the fact that, in a number of cases, the former colonial power continues for political reasons to purchase some primary products at above the world price.

Closely allied to the continuing trade and investment ties are the ties of technical assistance and the supply of skilled personnel. African nations after independence have needed more, not fewer, outside technicians to help them run their much-expanded administration and economy. Most newly independent nations show an immediate rise in the absolute number, if not the percentage, of non-Africans in the senior government service. In many cases, there is even a rise in the absolute number of the nationals of the former colonial power (more Frenchmen in service in Tunisia, more Englishmen in Ghana). Furthermore, both the British and French governments have evolved special schemes whereby their civil servants and military officers may be seconded to work for determinate periods with inde-

* Ghana and Nigeria are worried, for example, by the competitive advantage of the Ivory Coast and Cameroun in the sale of cocoa to Germany because of the EEC arrangements.

pendent African governments (former colonies) without
loss of pay or seniority in the metropolitan country.

Although there may be as many Europeans in African
independent nations today as there were before independence, or more, the turnover has often been very
large. They are different Europeans. Sometimes as
many as 80 percent have served in the independent
African country only since independence. Former officials have left because they could not accept the new
political climate or because they were asked to leave.
Others have gone because of exceptionally generous
offers of severance often made at the moment of independence. In many cases these offers allowed officials
in their middle years to obtain large grants as compensation, but only if they left immediately. As a compromise between the demands of Africanization and justice
to the overseas civil servant, these provisions have
often misfired, fulfilling neither goal adequately. Still
it is important to realize that a significant proportion
of senior civil servants in African independent nations
today come from the former colonial power, although
the number and percentage will decline as accelerated
programs of university education produce sufficient
graduates.

It can be seen that, even with independence, the
relation of former African colony to former European
colonial power still retains some of the flavor of province
and metropole. The strength of this bond, nevertheless, is uncertain. It is under severe attack by the more
militant pan-Africanists as "neo-colonialism." There is
no question that, even among those Africans who wish
to maintain their special relationship with the former
colonial power, there is a deeply felt desire to establish
ties with other nations and to lessen the dependence—
economic, political, and even cultural—on one power.
African nations are taking a number of specific steps·
to make this possible.

African independent nations are reaching out to es-

tablish new ties with both the United States and the
Soviet Union. In the case of the United States, these
contacts often are not new. The United States established diplomatic relations with the Sultanate of Morocco in the eighteenth century, and much of the
early diplomatic history of the United States revolves
around dealings with North Africa, with what were at
that time called the Barbary States. In the mid-nineteenth century, it was the efforts of the American
Colonization Society that led to the establishment of
the Republic of Liberia as a haven for liberated slaves.
Many Africans, therefore, at least in the past, have
considered Liberia an American colony for which the
United States bears a special responsibility. Henry
Stanley, journalist and explorer of the Congo, though
British by birth went to Africa on behalf of an American newspaper. Partly as a result of his activities, the
United States was involved in turning the Congo over
to King Leopold at the Congress of Berlin. The United
States was one of the signatories of the Berlin Conven-
tion that partitioned Africa (as, indeed, was Russia).

American missionaries have been in Africa, especially
the central and southern parts, from the mid-nineteenth
century. American Negro evangelists played some role
in the rise of African separatist movements, most
notably in the uprising of John Chilembwe in Nyasaland in 1915. And it is the American Negro Du Bois,
who is called the "father of pan-Africanism." In the
twentieth century, American business has entered into
the African market, particularly the mining industries
of the Union of South Africa, Northern Rhodesia and
Liberia (as well as rubber in Liberia).

African students have been coming to American
universities since the mid-nineteenth century. Many of
the leading nationalist leaders of English-speaking African states have studied in the United States, including two heads of state: Kwame Nkrumah, President of
Ghana, and Nnamdi Azikiwe, Governor-General of

Nigeria. One of the attractions of the United States for some African students has been that it is not an African colonial power and, despite race prejudice within the country, has had a reputation for anticolonialism on the international scene.

American contacts have been primarily with English-speaking Africa. First of all, there was no language problem. Furthermore, among the various colonial authorities, the British placed the fewest barriers in the way of contact between Americans and Africans. However, the Belgian Congo was officially a free trade area, and this meant that both businessmen and missionaries were allowed access. In Portuguese Africa, there were some missionaries. Perhaps the least contact was with French Africa, where even American consulates were discouraged, and from which no students ever went to the United States.

The reputation of the United States in Africa during the colonial era was a mixed one. It was composed of two central images: a tradition of anticolonialism, because the United States produced the first nationalist anticolonial revolution; a tradition of racism and lynching, which received wide coverage in whatever press existed in Africa. The balance of the two was considered somewhat more favorable in English-speaking Africa than in French Africa, perhaps because of the closer contact, which allowed the individual behavior of Americans (the informal, democratic mores) to be added to the scale. The period of decolonization after World War II saw a sharpening of this favorable image in the minds of Africans. There were also many improvements in race relations in the United States during this period. On the other hand, the anticolonial image was tarnished by United States hesitation to push the colonial powers on decolonization because of the Cold War (most notably, the North African and South African issues at the United Nations).

Nevertheless, one of the first steps of newly inde-

pendent African states has been to initiate or intensify
relations with the United States. In the case of French
black Africa, this contact amounts to a discovery of
a previously little-known quantity. The new contacts
sought are primarily economic and educational. African
states, attempting to industrialize, are seeking capital
from the United States government (the Volta River
Project in Ghana) and, in some cases, from private
investors as well (Fria in Guinea).* These nations are
also trying to send more students to the United States
and, in some cases, to obtain for African universities
and secondary schools American personnel and technical assistance.

This reaching out by African nations for international contacts applies to Western Europe generally as
well as to the United States. In the case of former
French colonies, this means contact with England; for
former British colonies, contact with France. In all
cases, contact with West Germany has been extensive,
particularly in terms of commerce and investment. The
story of new contact with the Western world also must
include a special word about Israel. Beginning in 1956,
the state of Israel made a special effort to establish
links with the newly independent states of black Africa,
even those which are predominantly Moslem. In this
attempt it has been somewhat successful since it combines three features particularly attractive to the new
African nations: it is a small power and therefore poses
little threat; it has available large numbers of skilled
technicians, whom it can lend to the African states; it
has a socialist ideology, and two unusual structures,
the kibbutz and the Histadrut, which Africans think
may have some relevance to their needs. Israel's success has been limited by the fact that she has been un-
willing openly to oppose France on the Algerian issue.
This reluctance, which derives from Israel's military

* Both the Volta River Project and Fria involve aid or investment from other than American sources as well.

need for French arms, has meant that Israel continues to be thought of as a European rather than as an Asian country, with all the psychological limitations such a denotation implies.

If, during the colonial era, contact of Africans with Americans was limited, it was infinitely more so with the Soviet Union. Historically, the ties between Russia and Africa were few,* and no colonial power gave any encouragement at all to African contact with a Communist state. There were occasional, relatively rare, instances before World War II of African students in Europe going to the USSR. After the Second World War, however, contacts with the Soviet Union began to increase, particularly those of French Africa, through the intermediary of international Communist-dominated nongovernmental groups (World Federation of Trade Unions, World Peace Movement, World Federation of Democratic Youth, etc.). Even so, part of the compromise of the dyarchy was to eliminate, or at least cut down, these contacts. Therefore, it is only with independence that real contact has been established, and even that has happened slowly. Nevertheless, the desire of the African states not merely to have contact with, but to receive economic aid and technical assistance from, the Soviet Union is genuine and growing and probably will become a normal feature of African political life.

In some ways, the Soviet Union is to Africans, particularly black Africans, simply another part of the Western world. It is China, not the USSR, that fascinates. China is not a white nation. It is more militant than the USSR on colonial questions. It is a poorer country, and its efforts at economic development are more relevant to Africa's problems, the Africans think. Above all, China has been a colony of the West, or at least a semi-colony. When Mao Tse-tung received an Algerian

* There were some ties, resuscitated recently, between the Russian Orthodox Church and the Coptic Church in Ethiopia.

delegation, he is reported to have said: "The Europeans and Americans despise you and they despise us. There are only 10 million of you and there are 600 million of us. But the bond that unites us is that we have both been humiliated, and this is a stronger bond than numbers." This bond has meant little as a concrete political or economic reality so far, but increasing links are to be expected. The work of the Afro-Asian Solidarity Council, in which the Chinese are very active, is the prelude of this increasing contact.

Africans also are seeking increasing contact with "the underdeveloped world," with Asia and Latin America. Japan is establishing commercial links with Africa. India, Ceylon and Indonesia are establishing political links, as are Cuba, Brazil and Mexico.

The very diversity of these new contacts testifies to the desire not to be enclosed in any limited Eurafrican framework, such as the proposed schemes that would bind Europe and Africa into a close economic community. For Eurafrica symbolizes neo-colonialism, and the rejection of neo-colonialism is what is meant by African neutralism. Neutralism is the determination to judge other countries by how they help solve African problems, the determination to be tied too closely to no one, and somewhat to everyone. Neutralism is indeed very closely linked with pan-Africanism. It is a means toward pan-Africanism. It is one of the ideological justifications for it since it is argued that a divided Africa will soon fall prey to a cold war polarization, whereas a united Africa will be strong enough to enforce its uniqueness and own interests. Neutralism serves African interests because it maximizes the possibilities of political maneuvers and the possibilities of economic assistance.

Neutralism is more than a doctrine that governs the foreign relations of African independent states. It affects the very nature of the political and economic doctrines that inspire the structures of the new nations.

We already have mentioned the fact that most African states speak of their goal as the establishment of socialism. The books they have read are either from the Marxist tradition or from the Catholic social tradition centering around Emmanuel Mounier's doctrine of "personalism" and the contemporary work of Father Lebret. The books they write, however, and the speeches they make, refer not to socialism but to "African socialism." The concept of "African socialism" is part of Africa's cultural revival, mentioned previously in Chapter VII, but we look at it here because of its implications for Africa's international relations.

African socialism is a doctrine defined in various ways by contemporary African thinkers. What they all have in common is the tendency to emphasize the point that African socialism is somehow distinctively African, rooted in African tradition, and therefore not intrinsically related to socialism anywhere else. The idea is usually expressed thus: Africans can learn much from the Soviet, Chinese, Scandinavian, British, Israeli, and Yugoslav varieties of socialism, but should adapt these techniques to African realities, using as a basis traditional African communal practices. Some few intellectuals oppose the adjective "African," arguing that socialism is a system of universal applicability. Usually these persons are referring to the Communist model. It is important to note that these few intellectuals are opposed systematically by the persons in power in all the African independent states. This is precisely because "African socialism" is set up as the alternative to "socialism," since the latter implies some sort of subordination to a non-African, largely European, doctrine and movement.

In particular, "African socialism" rejects the doctrine of the class struggle as inapplicable to the African situation since, it is argued, there are no classes in Africa. This argument is based on the fact that there are very few individual property owners who engage in business enterprise, also on the fact that there are very few persons in the liberal professions. The overwhelming proportion of the population are peasants. And, it is further contended, the small percentage of urbanites have not yet acquired a "bourgeois mentality." The evidence of this is their continued willingness to recognize obligations deriving from the extended kinship system, and the relative absence of class-based snobbery.

While observers may argue with the contention that one cannot speak of classes in a modern African nation —this is less true in some countries than in others— the contention serves some useful purposes. It underlines the priority of the national (political) struggle over any economic considerations. It is part of the ideological armory used by the nationalist party to help integrate the nation. For if there are no classes in Africa, then there is no reason to justify internal divisions. There is also no reason to justify an elite as opposed to a mass party. If there is only one class, the "class of the dispossessed," then the country as a whole, or Africa as a whole, has a claim against the more developed areas of the world. If Africa is already a classless society, then the corpus of Marxist analysis about the inevitable necessity of a further social revolution is denied, and the relevance of Communist doctrine to African problems becomes remote. Finally, as Sékou Touré has argued: "If we can demonstrate that without the class struggle a profound revolution is possible, we shall thus have begun the integration of Africa into the world of universal thought, to which she will have brought a new experience in the domain of political science and human action." Here we see how African neutralism leads us back to African cultural revival, each being the proud assertion of African uniqueness.

It is for these reasons that Communism, as a world movement, has had a smaller impact on Africa than on any other continent. Historically, there have been

official Communist parties only in Morocco, Algeria,
Tunisia, Egypt, and the Union of South Africa.* It is
no accident that these countries (except Egypt) are
the settler extremities of Africa. For in French North
Africa and in the Union of South Africa it was largely
persons of European descent who formed the cadres
and the membership of the Communist parties. This
reinforced the impression that Communism was external European doctrine.

The struggle to create unified nationalist movements
in African countries was not merely a matter of over-
coming procolonial groupings among the population. It
also involved breaking with the Communist movements. This was particularly true in the French areas
where, between 1950 and 1957, the major political
party in French black Africa, the trade unions in
French North Africa, and the trade unions in French
West Africa broke their links with Communist movements as a means of asserting their autonomy. Since
independence, this rejection has been reasserted many
times. Even those countries most vigorously reaching
out for contacts with the Soviet Union and China on a
governmental level are very restrictive internally with
Communist movements. The UAR continues to keep
leading Communists in jail. Guinea and Mali have
refused to allow the Parti Africain de l'Indépendence,
a Marxist-Leninist party, to operate within its borders.
Sékou Touré has also declared that Communists are
not welcome as members of the governing Parti Démocratique de Guinée. Indeed, the stronger and more
neutralist the party in power in Africa, the more effective have been the barriers to the formation of Communist parties because the doctrine of African neutral-

* These parties are presently outlawed everywhere except in
Tunisia. The Communist party of the Sudan has never been
legal. A party was formed in Somalia in 1956 (but not officially
recognized) and in Madagascar in 1958.

ism has shown itself essentially hostile to subordination to a European ideology.

The population of Africa is very small in proportion to the rest of the world. Yet Africa plays a role in world politics out of proportion to its size. Its importance is partly a function of its turbulence, but even more a function of its vigorous autonomism, its intense desire to eliminate all vestiges of foreign control, however disguised. This desire for autonomy is not unique, but it is found in Africa in a very concentrated form.

:IX:

PROSPECTS

FOR DEMOCRACY

In the ten years following World War II, there were perhaps two major views of the African political scene held by outsiders and to a considerable extent by Africans themselves. One view held that Africans were incapable or not yet capable of exercising responsible self-rule and creating modern, democratic societies. Originally, this was a majority point of view but it has rapidly declined in acceptance until only a small group of impenitent white settlers still cling to it. A second view was that the nationalist anticolonial revolution would lead to the establishment of parliamentary democracies of a Western style, dominated by a small but growing middle class, reasonably devoted to the defense of civil liberties. This view was particularly popular amongst Western "liberals" who supported African nationalism. This view was shared, however, by Marxist analysts, with the difference that the latter often saw the development of a bourgeois democracy as an essentially unstable transitional stage on the road to communist society. Most African nationalists would have proferred the same analysis of what would occur after independence.

Yet by 1960 not only had both points of view been belied but there were few persons left, certainly few Africans left, who could be found to put forward these arguments. Indeed, what had happened was that African nationalists had begun to proclaim as valid the kinds of institutions which were in fact coming into existence in the newly independent states of Africa. They were no longer ashamed of the fact that these institutions bore only an outward resemblance to the Western parliamentary system. On the contrary, they now proclaimed these institutions as a peculiarly African contribution to the theory of *democratic* society.

It is important to appreciate that African nationalists make a clear distinction in their own minds between parliamentary institutions and "democracy." This is a distinction not unknown to Western political thought. It has been rediscovered by contemporary African statesmen, who almost unanimously are building their state structures on a model they might admit was neither liberal nor individualistic but which they would insist was "democratic."

We have previously noted the tendency of independent African states to have a single-party political system, or at least a single-dominant-party one. We have analyzed how the need of a new nation to maintain its territory and enhance the loyalty of its citizens accounts for this tendency. We have furthermore discussed the special role of the national hero in this transitional phase of African history. It is not surprising, then, that Africans create ideological justifications for the structures they find necessary to resolve their primary problems.

Multi-party systems have often been considered indispensable to a democratic society on the theory that freedom involves the possibility of choice between alternative groups, each being a separate set of men with a particular program, presumably different from that of any other group. Heroes have always been suspect

in the eyes of supporters of democracy on the theory
that they resemble absolute monarchs in potentially
being able to impose their will arbitrarily (or by il-
legitimate emotional appeals) on the majority of the
population. Single parties and heroes have often been
assumed to lead to dictatorships whereby a small group
of men effectively dominate the society.

What in fact is the situation after independence?
What are the possibilities for dissent and free discussion? What degree of protection does the individual
citizen have against the arbitrary decisions of those in
power? To what degree is decision-making a collective
process, or rather are decisions based on consensus or
imposed rule? The situation obviously varies from state
to state and from one point in time to another. Nevertheless, we can detect a general pattern which holds for
most independent African states within a certain range
of variance.

Most independent African states have one form or
another of preventive detention acts.* These acts are
quite often the direct inheritance of the colonial situation, and are now used in behalf of those against whom
they were originally directed. Most states (for example,
Sudan, Upper Volta, Niger, Ghana, Gabon) not only
have these acts; they use them. The justifications the
governments usually offer is that the persons detained
are "unconstructively in the opposition," that is, they
are engaged in activities tending toward the disintegration of the nation, sometimes actual secession. Emergency powers allowing special restrictions, also have
been voted for governments. This is most notably true
of Cameroun, where a civil war continued after independence because, with the coöperation of the French,

* This is in fact true of many states throughout the world. Even
the so-called traditional democracies have such acts in times of
emergency: for example, in the United States, the Japanese
Relocation Act in World War II; in France, the special powers
voted to the French government during the Algerian War.

the core of the original nationalist movement was
excluded from power.

In many cases, preventive detention has seemed inadequate to governments, and they therefore have
resorted to deportations. The deportations might be of
high-level political leaders born in other countries, as
in the case of the 1958 expulsions from the Republic of
Mali, Upper Volta, Guinea, Niger, or in Chad in 1960.
Sometimes these would be of middle-level opposition
leaders who were "foreigners" (Ghana in 1957) or
even locally born (Ivory Coast in 1959). But there has
been another kind of "deportation" as well, the encouraged departure of a whole segment of the population: the Guinean diamond seekers from Sierra Leone,
the Dahomean and Togolese civil servants from the
Ivory Coast and Niger. In the case of the Dahomeans
in the Ivory Coast, the expulsion was the result of
popular riots, to which the government acceded. In
the case of Sierra Leone, it was a government-initiated
move to crack down on illicit diamond mining.

There has been considerable manipulation with the
electoral laws aimed at eliminating small opposition
parties from seats in legislative bodies. Under the British colonial regime, most legislative bodies were elected
on a single-member constituency regime. Under the
French regime, a portion of the constituencies were
single-member. This made it more difficult at first for
the nationalist party to win seats, as there were always
rural areas in which the party was weak and the seat
could be a fief of the local traditional ruler who was
friendly to the colonial administration.

In the time of the dyarchy, many of the African states
began to adopt systems of multi-member constituencies.
This was particularly true in French Africa. One of the
arguments advanced was that only in this way was it
possible for the nationalist party to overcome tribal
commitments. In multi-member constituencies, a party
could present candidates simultaneously from several
tribes. Furthermore, during the dyarchy, it was often

the policy to elect a few Europeans on the nationalist
ticket. Single-member constituencies would have been
inappropriate for this purpose. Of course, multi-member constituencies could be run either on a majority
vote (winner takes all) or proportional basis, which as-
sures minority representation. There was a strong tendency toward the majority vote system.

As time went on, the number of constituencies was
successively reduced, the number of legislators to be
elected in each being increased. By the 1959 elections
in French Africa, for example, most states had reduced
the number of constituencies to four and six, Mauritania to only two. This practically assured the majority
party all the seats. There were some few states where
the opposition party was particularly strong in one
region, and could win one constituency, however large
it was made. Thereupon, to eliminate this group, a
final step was taken in 1961 in Dahomey, Togo, and
Gabon: in each case the whole nation became a single
constituency. One vote of the voter elected a list, including the president of the republic and all the members
of parliament.

These obvious manipulations are necessary to eliminate opposition groups. Once they are eliminated,
however, multi-member constituencies remain as an
aid to the process of national integration. However, it
probably is useful also to have a number of constituencies in order to provide intermediate points of regional
attachment between the individual and the state. A
mild version of regionalism may serve to relieve the
pressures of local demands.

If manipulation of the electoral laws is insufficient
to assure the one-party state, other mechanisms are
available. African governments have outlawed parties,
or refused recognition* to parties newly created, for

* Under most African legal systems, political parties must
register with the government, and can only operate once their
legality is recognized. This arrangement is a heritage of the
colonial administration.

example, in Morocco, Sudan, the UAR, Senegal, Mauritania, Upper Volta, Niger, Mali, Cameroun, the Central African Republic. Another way of eliminating opposition members from parliament is by simple expulsion. The justification may be preventive detention, or charges of falsified election procedures, or the outlawing of the party to which the parliamentarian belongs. There have been instances of such expulsion in Chad, Niger, Togo, Ghana, the Central African Republic.

To achieve some of these objectives, African governments have tended to treat lightly the question of the independence of the judiciary. Sometimes they have openly demanded that political considerations take priority for judges over legal considerations. Sometimes the legislatures simply by statute have overridden unfavorable judicial decisions. Governments have felt free to alter constitutional provisions that created obstacles to immediate goals, and with their overwhelming majorities in the legislative bodies, they have had no trouble acquiring the extra vote necessary for constitutional amendment. The concern for substantive as against procedural justice has been made central by the new African governments. The protections of form and due process are feared by these governments because a system which places great emphasis on these protections works on the assumption that the individual exercises certain restraints in his actions toward the state. We have seen previously that this is not yet true, and that African governments are working hard to achieve this kind of national integration. It should not be surprising, therefore, that until this sense of self-restraint permeates the citizenry, the government should be reluctant to allow the liberties of due process their full play.

Another form of restriction in the one-party state is that related to voluntary associations. There has been considerable pressure to keep them in line with the position of the party. When these groups have deviated sharply, they have been pressured, either by purges inspired by the party, or by withdrawal of financial and other aid by the government. Instances include the trade unions in Tunisia and Senegal, the women's organizations in Ghana, the youth councils in Senegal and Niger, the students' organizations in Guinea, Mali, and the Ivory Coast.

We see, then, that the newly independent African states are not models of liberalism. It is important to note, from the examples given above, that this non-democratic tendency is a very general phenomenon. It is not limited to states with a particular colonial tradition. It has nothing to do with the attitudes of the government toward pan-Africanism or the East-West issue. It is almost universal since it results from the similar needs of national unity and economic development that all these countries face. The one important exception thus far has been Nigeria. In Nigeria, there are three regions, each with a dominant party. Were those regions independent states, there is little reason to suppose each would not have evolved along the lines of its neighbors. Because they are in a federal structure without any effective national party in existence, no group has been able to engage in electoral manipulation, expulsions, deportations, and detentions—at least not to the extent of other states. Because no one has a clear majority at the federal level, each party can protect its friends in the other regions. Whether this situation will last indefinitely remains to be seen.

Although African independent states are not liberal in their practices, they are by no means totalitarian. The citizens do not live in terror of a secret police. Political debate is a commonplace of African life. Opposition to government policies exists, is heard, is even listened to. Policies change; the composition of governments changes. There is an enormous amount of give and take in almost every independent African state.

How is it possible at one and the same time not to
have liberal political structures in the African states
and yet to have many of the presumed consequences of
liberal political structures? One explanation is that the
intensive political concern which African nationalist
movements created as part of the struggle for independence has bequeathed an atmosphere in which popular participation in political matters is still considered
the normal thing. At national elections, it is quite common to have turnouts of 80 to 90 percent. Nationalist
movements cannot simply at will turn on and off this
enthusiasm for mass involvement in the political arena,
even if they want to. And indeed, as we have seen, they
do not want to. For popular participation is one of the
tools the party uses to achieve national integration. In
those states where the party structure is best articulated, mass membership in the party means that party
meetings at the village level resemble "town meetings."
This is of course an ideal situation, and in many African
countries, this ideal is not achieved.

Mass participation in itself would not be significant
were there not a climate in which free discussion is encouraged. Such a climate does exist today in most of
the new states, insofar as such discussion is kept within
the framework of the party structure. This is a limitation, to be sure, but not one that eliminates the reality
of debate. There is no single-party structure in African
independent states where the observer cannot identify
factions and tendencies which argue with each other to
some extent over issues. The parliamentary structures,
even if one party has all the seats, are not entirely
docile. Debate is spirited, and the voice of the back-
bencher is often heard. Indeed, there are instances
where the open revolt of government backbenchers
(Ghana, Gabon) have forced the government to change
its views.

It must be remembered that these single-party structures are not integrated organisms but integrating or-

ganisms. That is, they are carefully built coalitions, in need of constant nurture, whose primary aim is to keep the country together. The principal method of maintaining party unity, indispensable to national unity, is the constant balancing of interests. The allocation of seats in the legislature, or expenditures of the public works department, are the result of hard bargaining and careful calculation, which bear comparison with the interplay of special interests in Western parliaments. The image of a small elite imposing their will, through the party structure, on an inert mass fails to take account of the real dispersion of power that still exists in every African country.

The national hero is not a dictator who reigns by whim and fiat. He tends to be the spokesman of, probably the dominating figure in, a national political bureau of a political party. He is the chairman of the inner policy debates, which go on constantly. He is the mediator of the various political factions, the different ethnic and religious groups. He is, as Africans tend to call their chiefs, "the grandfather." He is exalted, to be sure, because his glorification serves the purpose of helping to create a nation. He is exalted, too, because he then can become a symbol of African achievement in the wider world, the proof that African states can produce statesmen and heroes to match those of the rest of the world. But his independence of action tends to be very rigidly constrained by the party of which he is the leader, and the nation which he must bind together.

The possibilities of discussion within the party and the limitations on the power of the leader are not guaranteed by legal protection for the opposition or the institutions of a multi-party system. They are not, however, without any cultural support. There are two major underpinnings for this continued democratic atmosphere. One is the African tradition of government. While this is less true in Arab Africa than in black

Africa, the traditional structures of government in
Africa are built on the principles of debate and consensus, with the chief as mediator and transmitter of
the will of his councilors. The tradition requires too
that the councilors be drawn from the various segments
of the community. In most cases, succession to the
throne is not automatic but involves a choice by the
councilors, and often by the people, of one candidate
from among a large group of eligible persons. There is a
remarkable similarity between these familiar traditional ways and the formulas that in fact govern the
newly independent national governments.

It is not only African tradition that protects dissent
and discussion in Africa today. There are also more
modern factors which contribute to this result. One is
the continued turmoil and movement of the African
political scene. Nationalist struggle has been succeeded
by pan-Africanism to assure constant change, political
maneuver, realignment. The arteries of political activity
have scarcely been permitted to harden anywhere.
Such constant agitation requires an atmosphere in
which ideas can be constantly debated, in which the
angers of the moment are not allowed to become permanent enmities; it requires that each government keep
in reserve men to implement new policies. At least thus
far it has been so.

Furthermore, the ceaseless onrush of political happenings has meant that inter-African structures and
contacts have continued to be significant in the political
life of any given African country. Ideas have constantly
flowed across frontiers—dissenting ideas. And because
pan-Africanism has been so strong a sentiment, men
and parties have constantly intervened in the affairs
of other African states to protect those who shared
their point of view. What has guaranteed the give and
take of African politics to some extent has been the
fact that no African state has lived within itself but
each has been very much a part of a wider African

movement. To the degree that inter-African exchange has been characteristic of a given state, the free interchange of ideas within that state has been possible.

The assessment of the degree of democracy in African states must be based on an appreciation of the alternatives that exist. The choice is not between a one-party system and a multi-party parliamentary system. The structural prerequisites for the latter do not yet exist to a sufficient degree in Africa. The effective choice for the newly independent states is between a one-party (or one-dominant-party) system, which allows for some real popular participation in, and control over, the government, or anarchy, which means that power reverts to local princelings and patrons, remote from the intellectual contact and stimulation which infuses the modernizing elite of the national structures.

The one-party system in the African context is often a significant step toward the liberal state, not a first step away from it. For the purpose of the one-party system is to create a national state sufficiently well-rooted in the loyalties of its citizens so that the distinction between state and government will begin to emerge. Without this basic loyalty, the relative stability of the state cannot be assumed, and governments will continue to refuse to tolerate opposition that is not contained within their own party, for fear that such opposition will lead to the dismantlement of the state. This fear is not wholly without foundation.

The national orientation of the mass of citizens is not the sole prerequisite for the creation of institutions that can guarantee the rights of opposition, even outside the party. African states, as we have seen, are determined to raise their economic level by industrializing and by mechanizing their agriculture. The point of economic development is to achieve greater equality with the rest of the world, as well as to further the integration of the nation. A developed economy creates a new pattern of social strata. Occupational and income groupings become more nearly balanced. The disproportion of a situation where 95 percent of the population are peasant farmers disappears. As this new stratification develops, the interest groupings of citizens become defined largely in terms of these economic and occupational roles. But these groupings tend to be nationwide rather than regional in scope, which the present groupings based on ethnic considerations usually are. As interests become nationwide, opposition will cease to lead to territorial secession, since territorial secession will then usually be irrelevant to the political objectives of the opposition.

Dissent and discussion in African states today are guaranteed in part by African tradition, in part by the continued political turmoil. These are not longterm guarantees, since tradition is being weakened and turmoil may cease. The one-party systems may begin to stagnate without any internal structural protection for the opposition (independent judiciary, free press, etc.). This is clearly a danger of the future. Yet these structural guarantees will not be acceptable as long as they threaten the preservation of the state. The building up of loyalty to the nation, combined with the economic differentiation that development will bring, plus the resulting creation of nationwide interest groups will create a situation in which the institution of structural guarantees will no longer threaten the preservation of the state.

It does not follow, however, that these structural guarantees will thereupon be instituted. The emergence of long-range institutional guarantees of a democratic society is by no means automatic. However, it is not really possible at all before the prerequisites are fulfilled. The problem therefore is twofold: how to fulfill the prerequisites as rapidly as possible, and how to do so in such a way as to maximize the possibility that the authoritarian regimes of the present will not stagnate

and harden but will develop further toward the increase
of personal freedom within the state.

All those steps which promote national unity are
therefore steps in this direction. Pressure for formal
constitutional guarantees and outward conformity to
parliamentary norms, if premature, may only lead to
the breakdown of these institutions, as has occurred
in a number of Asian countries, and consequent disillusion with the usefulness of such institutions *at any
time*. On the other hand, entry of the opposition into
the government and the machinery of the governing
party not only serves the interests of unity, but usually,
though not always, helps to maintain within the dominant party openness of discussion and the necessary
pressures for arriving at a consensus that takes into
account all interests.

Rapid economic development too moves in this direction, and rapid economic development is tied to national integration, simultaneously as cause and consequence. Those processes that aid national integration—
strengthening the party structure, creating inter-African unities, or obtaining international aid from a variety of sources—all help the states pass through the
transitional postindependence phase as rapidly as possible.

Since among the factors which preserve the present
flow of ideas and discussion in Africa today are the
inter-African links, it follows that insofar as these links
expand or take more concrete political form, the climate
remains attuned to liberal norms and formal guarantees
of dissent. Thus, the movement for African unity, both
by improving the prospects of economic development
and by widening the channels of communication and
sources of ideas, strengthens democratic mores in Africa.

What is true of inter-African links is true of wider
international links. Increased familiarity and contact
with the vast panorama of variant conditions and polit-

ical structures on the world scene should make for subtler and more tolerant analyses of problems and their solutions. Given the strong sense of African autonomism, reinforced as it continues to be by pan-African trends, increased contacts not only with the United States and the Soviet Union, but with Europe, Asia, and Latin America are moves toward the creation of an interwoven mosaic, which encourages flexibility of tactics and ideas, and serves to moderate the extremism of all. The transitional era of African life coincides with a transitional era of the world polity in which the polarized structure of international politics is being attenuated. Of course, world tensions may increase, despite the decolonization process, in which case the internal structure of African states will become tighter instead of more flexible.

The one-party structure is an interim system of African states which they are maintaining for the present. And with the one-party structure goes, as we have seen, the continued politicization of the voluntary associations on the African scene, the continued domination of trade unions, youth groups, women's associations, etc., by the mass political party. Yet, with an eye to the future, the separate existence of these functional groups, no matter how dependent currently on the party, cannot but serve the end of political diversification. Youth and trade union structures may be required to subordinate their special interests today to the national views of the party. But by maintaining and extending their separate structures, they may, when the moment is ripe, serve as the bases of separate political groupings, even parties. Many African trade unionists, therefore, prefer to restrain their demands today, the better to be in position to put them forward tomorrow. Also, the wider links which these groups have, through inter-African and international trade union (or youth or women's) organizations, serve to strengthen their own positions internally vis-à-vis the

party structure, as well as allow these groups to be the
initiators of ideas and methods other than those taught
within the state.

All of this patient contact and rapid integration and
economic growth may not pay off in terms of the insti-
tutionalization of devices that protect and stimulate
dissent unless the currents of intellectual life are strong
and original. Here too, pan-Africanism can have a
healthy influence, as can the multiplication of sources
of intellectual stimulation (an opinion press, universities, seminars which bring together politicians and
intellectuals). The serious intellectual discussion of African and human problems by Africans, among themselves and with others, is a key to political evolution,
and is by no means incompatible with the present
trends toward one-party states, cultural revival, and
pan-Africanism.

A democratic society, in Africa as elsewhere, depends
on a certain climate of opinion. This climate of opinion
can only be maintained in the long run if it is supported
by the norms of the society, reinforced by appropriate
structural protections, defended in turn by significant
strata of the population who have a positive interest
in, and relatively little fear of, dissent. The independent
African states are moving in this direction in ways not
unlike those which other states used in comparable
periods of their nation-building.

Africa has greatness in her past as well as her present.
And probably in her future too.

EPILOGUE

Looking at

African Independence

Ten Years Later

Books should be read and assessed as a reflection of their time. My own book is very much a book of the early 1960's. I wrote it for the most part in the fall of 1960 and I had a chance to make corrections up through the late spring of 1961.

I remember 1960 as a moment of great optimism and renewal, both in Africa and in the United States. In Africa, 1960 was the Year of Independence, the year in which the All-African Peoples' Conference meeting in Tunis had set 1963 as a deadline for the total liberation of Africa. Africans did not think this date fanciful, and I for one shared their optimism. One of the most egregious errors of the book occurs on page 6, where I said: "As of the writing of this book, it seems likely that the remaining nonindependent states will become independent within several years." The year 1963 was chosen as the deadline, incidentally, because it marked the 100th anniversary of the Emancipation Proclamation—which tells us something of Africa's relationship to the United States in 1960.

In the United States, 1960 was the year John F. Kennedy was elected President. It is easy now to see the Kennedy era as simply one more step in a long and consistent march of American politics. I myself have recently argued this in an article in *Africa Report* on

American foreign policy in Africa. But at the time,
Kennedy seemed to promise a breath of fresh air in the
musty atmosphere of Cold War thinking. Those of us
who lived through the 1950's—whose oppressiveness
was more intellectual and less physical than that of
some other eras—thought there was a chance for significant social change in America through peaceful
means. It was not that we had any blind faith in
Kennedy as an individual—the Kennedy myth starts
largely with his assassination—but that Kennedy's
regime seemed to reflect some social changes that were
occurring elsewhere in the country and the world:
de-Stalinization in the USSR, Castro's coming to power
in Cuba, the civil rights movement in the United States.

No doubt all of this facile optimism was unfounded
and led us into error. But I find it easy to understand
how both Africa and the United States could have
jumped so eagerly and enthusiastically on this band-
wagon of hope after difficult years of struggle both had
known just before, and I put forth no *mea culpa* for
being optimistic and acting politically and intellectually
in terms of it.

So much for background. What of the book? Do I still
defend its theses, now that I am more sober about what
was going on then, now that I have revised my judgment
of many events that happened between 1945 and 1960,
both in Africa and in the United States?

Let me start by outlining the three most important
lacunae or underemphases in the book which I have
thought about and written about in the years since 1961.
The first concerns the colonial period in its prime; the
second, the period of decolonization; the third, the
politics of the immediate postindependence period.

My discussion of social change in the colonial era
placed too little emphasis on the widespread, continuing
phenomenon of rural discontent. One or two critics and
colleagues, particularly Herbert Weiss, picked me up on
this, in print and in private. But my critics were sur-

prisingly few in number. It is easy now to see why this should have been so. Because my generation of American scholars were so upset by how the early (British) anthropologists had concentrated their attention on the rural areas, in a search for pristine, ahistorical tribal cultures, and ignored, along with the colonial administrators, the new educated classes, we failed to notice that the error of the anthropologists was not that they studied the rural areas, but *how* they studied them. It became the destiny of a subsequent wave of social science writing, especially that of the new breed of Afrocentric historians, such as the so-called Dar es Salaam school of Terence Ranger and his colleagues, to begin to rectify this particular imbalance.

It seems clear to me now, as I have since stated, that the colonial order was very disorderly indeed; that peasant rebelliousness, if sporadic, was unceasing; and that the discontent of the urban educated classes can neither be understood nor evaluated properly without putting it in the context of rural turmoil.

The second way in which my book was deficient grows out of the first limitation. I presented the process of decolonization in Africa as a political compromise, entered into by the two main parties represented at the negotiating tables: the metropolitan governments and the nationalist leadership. I argued that there came a point where each side, in its calculus of interests, perceived such a compromise as beneficial. I still believe this to be correct. However, what I did not stress sufficiently at the time, and have since made explicit in later work, is the degree to which this compromise was made at the expense of lower strata of the society (that is, small farmers, landless agricultural labor, unskilled and semiskilled urban workers, the unemployed school-leavers). Not only was this compromise made at their expense. It was intended to be at their expense. The metropolitan powers were making concessions in order to separate the nationalist leadership from these strata

and prevent a more coherent and conscious degree of
radical political activity; most of the nationalist elite
were either indifferent to the needs of these strata or
explicitly frightened of the potential threat to their own
positions. In partial self-defense, I might say that in
1960 most of the more radical members of the African
elites were not yet able or willing to openly criticize their
peers. They feared that a split in the African "united
front" could set back the granting of independence.
Neocolonial compromise though some thought it to be,
these same persons preferred obtaining the legal appurtenances of sovereignty to remaining still longer
under colonial rule. And I have always felt that it is
wrong to be more royalist than the king.

The third limitation to my argument is that my picture of the one-party system and the national hero is
somewhat rosy, as many said at the time of first pub-
lication. Only, I'm not sure I mean rosy in the same way
many of my critics did. The way I feel it was rosy is
precisely the consequence of the second lacuna. I did not
stress the degree to which the single-party system, in
most cases, was, in Fanon's phrase, a dictatorship of the
bourgeoisie. I have since done so. I have also since
stressed the degree to which the party in the one-party
state tends to become a ceremonial institution subordinate to the state machinery.

In addition, I overestimated the staying power of
national heroes—even those who were real ones, in the
sense both of their historic role and strength of personality. It is encouraging morally and intellectually to
see that even men of impressive acumen, foresight and
political courage—I count Nkrumah among them—are
creatures rather than creators of their society, and that
once, for whatever reason, they no longer reflect the
confluence of social forces, once they make too many
"mistakes," they fall. I am not applauding their fall.
On the contrary. But I am noting that the element of
personal strength which they intrude on the political

equation—their "charisma," if you will, that now perhaps discarded phrase—is fragile and conjunctural.

Having noted the ways in which I would amend or
add to my arguments as I originally presented them,
let me underline the aspects of the book I would most
emphatically reaffirm. I will do this in tandem with the
lacunae: one concerning the colonial period in its prime;
one concerning the period of decolonization; one concerning the politics of the immediate postindependence
period.

I presented the colonial period as a "colonial situation," that is, as one in which the territory (and, I
should add, at another level of analysis, the empire)
was a single arena of power and social action, within
which the phenomena we studied took place. Moreover,
this arena, this system, was beset by flagrant and
inherent contradictions that led to its early demise.
J. F. Ade Ajayi and other African historians are now
reminding us regularly how short the colonial period
was. They are trying to place into a longer African time-
perspective the importance of the impact of the colonial
rule. But the shortness points to a second truth: how
deeply unstable the particular form of social organization of a territory known as colonial rule really is.
Today, this way of looking at the colonial system as an
interacting totality is so widespread as to be often
implicit and unself-conscious. In 1960 the shadow of
Malinowski still loomed large.

I presented the process of decolonization as a sort of
carefully articulated minuet with few surprises and little
violence—which I still feel is a correct description of
what happened (outside of southern Africa). Even
Algeria and Kenya do not invalidate this description,
as the violence there was an integral part of the con-
tinent-wide minuet. The two wars were intensive but,
in important ways, constrained and predictable in their
evolution. I attributed the phenomenon of rapid, relatively easy decolonization to a conjuncture of the

world system, the Cold War between the United States and the Soviet Union. The impact of this international context on the principal negotiators of decolonization was, it seemed to me and still does, clear and direct—and indeed conscious and visible. To be sure, this conjuncture came to an end. In my second volume, *Africa: The Politics of Unity*, I dated the end as 1963, and explained how the end of the Cold War had very negatively affected the movement for African unity, the liberation of southern Africa and the economic development of the continent.

Finally, I presented the politics of the early post-independence period as one in which the one-party state was a central political mechanism. One colleague told me that the most "outrageous" statement I had made in my book was that found on page 96: "The choice has not been between one-party and multi-party states; it has been between one-party states and either anarchy or military regimes or various combinations of the two." Ten years later, this statement does not strike me as the least bit outrageous. I would say it has proved to be very accurate. I would go further. The only useful political analysis is to uncover what alternatives are in fact available for the actors in a given system at a given point of time. I argued then and would argue now that among the possible political forms which African states can take in the *present* era—that is, let us say, from 1957 to 1975—is neither the bourgeois liberal state (despite the romantic notions of the framers of the post-Nkrumah Ghana constitution), nor a state which would cut off all its economic links with the capitalist world (despite the wistful critiques of some non-African Marxists). I do not suggest that the latter is not possible in the foreseeable future. In fact, I have several times suggested that Nigeria, Congo/K and a post-revolution South Africa are all prime candidates for such a regime—not *now*, but *perhaps* ten to twenty years from now. I believed and believe that in the present period the one-

party system, to the extent that it can be effectively
established, is more viable and more beneficial to Africa
and to the world than any present alternative—this
despite all its shortcomings, cruelties and deceptions.

There is one other statement I made about the one-
party state which I should like to reaffirm and which
partially compensates for some of the lacunae I have
discussed. It is on page 161: "The image of a small elite
imposing their will, through the party structure, on an
inert mass fails to take account of the real dispersion of
power that still exists in every African country." Everything we have seen since 1960 reinforces this point. But
it is well perhaps to underline once more its theoretical
importance. We talk of systems, of institutions, of
influence. All these words exaggerate the articulation of
the structures and do not sufficiently evoke the image
of rumbling forces beneath the surface which are far
more determinative of the present and the future than
the things that are immediately apparent.

APPENDIX

Country	Capital	Area (sq. mi.)	Population	Year of Independence
INDEPENDENT STATES (1971)				
Algeria	Algiers	919,520	12,943,000	1962
Botswana	Gaberone	275,000	629,000	1966
Burundi	Bujumbura	10,740	3,406,000	1962
Cameroun	Yaoundé	183,380	5,562,000	1960
Central African Republic	Bangui	238,000	1,518,000	1960
Chad	Fort-Lamy	495,750	3,361,000	1960
Congo (former French Congo)	Brazzaville	132,050	10,730,000	1960
Congo (former Belgian Congo)	Kinshasa	905,380	16,730,000	1960
Dahomey	Porto-Novo	44,290	2,571,000	1960
Equatorial Guinea	Santa Isabel	10,850	286,000	1968
Ethiopia	Addis Ababa	443,350	23,900,000	B.C.
Gabon	Libreville	102,320	480,000	1960
Gambia	Bathurst	4,000	357,000	1965
Ghana	Accra	92,100	8,376,000	1957
Guinea	Conakry	96,865	3,702,000	1958
Ivory Coast	Abidjan	127,520	4,200,000	1960
Kenya	Nairobi	224,960	10,209,000	1963
Lesotho	Maseru	11,710	1,000,000	1966
Liberia	Monrovia	43,000	1,130,000	1847
Libya	Tripoli	679,400	1,869,000	1951
Malagasy Rep.	Tananarive	227,900	6,643,000	1960
Malawi	Zomba	49,000	4,285,000	1964
Mali	Bamako	463,500	4,900,000	1960
Mauritania	Nouakchott	418,810	1,120,000	1960
Mauritius	Port Louis	720	810,000	1968
Morocco	Rabat	172,100	14,817,000	1956
Niger	Niamey	494,000	3,909,000	1960
Nigeria	Lagos	356,670	62,650,000	1960
Rwanda	Kigali	10,170	3,306,000	1962
Senegal	Dakar	76,080	3,685,000	1960
Sierra Leone	Freetown	27,925	2,475,000	1961
Somalia	Mogadiscio	246,000	1,120,000	1960

INDEPENDENT STATES (1971)—*Continued*

Country	Capital	Area (sq. mi.)	Population	Year of Independence
South Africa	Pretoria	472,685	19,167,000	1910
Sudan	Khartoum	967,500	14,979,000	1956
Swaziland	Mbabane	6,700	375,000	1968
Tanzania	Dar es Salaam	363,330	12,926,000	1961*
Togo	Lomé	21,850	1,818,000	1960
Tunisia	Tunis	63,080	4,533,000	1956
Uganda	Kampala	93,980	8,133,000	1962
United Arab Republic	Cairo	363,000	31,680,000	1922
Upper Volta	Ouagadougou	105,900	5,278,000	1960
Zambia	Lusaka	290,320	4,144,000	1964

*Tanganyika became independent in 1961, Zanzibar in 1964; the two countries merged as the United Republic of Tanzania in 1964.

NONINDEPENDENT TERRITORIES (1971)

Country	Capital	Area (sq. mi.)	Population
FRANCE			
Comoro Islands	Dzaudzi	860	250,000
French Terr. of the Afars and Issas	Djibouti	9,070	125,000
Réunion	St. Denis	970	418,000
GREAT BRITAIN			
Southern Rhodesia*	Salisbury	150,000	4,740,000
PORTUGAL			
Angola (incl. Cabinda)	Luanda	481,350	5,293,000
Cape Verde Islands	Praia	1,560	232,000
Mozambique	Lourenço Marques	297,730	7,124,000
Portuguese Guinea	Bissau	13,950	528,000
Saõ Tomé e Príncipe	Saõ Tomé	372	60,000
SPAIN			
Spanish possessions in North Africa		82	156,000
Spanish Sahara	Aiún	105,560	48,000
UNITED NATIONS			
Namibia†	Windhoek	319,260	594,000

*Unilateral declaration of independence as Rhodesia in 1965; no international recognition.

†Mandate of South Africa revoked by United Nations in 1966; still under *de facto* control of South Africa under the name of South West Africa

BIBLIOGRAPHICAL NOTE

In the first edition (1961) I wrote: "The library of books about Africa is a fast-growing one." It has now grown to be an immense literature. Instead of trying to summarize it, let me indicate some starting points, which could lead the reader on to where he wants to go.

African history from the Australopithecines to today has perhaps expanded most of all. Two introductory surveys available in paperback are Basil Davidson, *Lost Cities of Africa*, revised edition, and Roland Oliver and J. D. Fage, *A Short History of Africa*. For those who wish to move one step beyond, there are now various collections of essays and comprehensive surveys by the specialists. These include the two-volume *History of East Africa*, edited by Roland Oliver and Gervase Matthew; the two-volume *Oxford History of South Africa*, edited by Monica Wilson and Leonard Thompson; the two-volume *Colonialism in Africa, 1870–1960*, edited by L. H. Gann and Peter Duignan; and the forthcoming two-volume *Oxford History of West Africa*, edited by J. F. Ade Ajayi and Michael Crowder. There are also two first-rate journals in the field: the *Journal of African History* and, for more recent material, the *Journal of Modern African Studies*.

In addition, for what went on in the colonial period, it is still useful to look at two famous compendia: R. L. Buell, *The Native Problem in Africa*, 2 vols., written in 1928, and Lord Hailey, *An African Survey*, revised in 1956. Thomas Hodgkin's early book (1955), *Nationalism in Colonial Africa*, remains a gem, and Rupert Emerson's *From Empire to Nation: The Rise of Self-*

Assertion of Asian and African Peoples is a good com-
plement to it.

The economies of contemporary Africa are a long
story. If one wants all the basic data, they are most
readily available in William A. Hance, *The Geography
of Modern Africa*. For some analysis of policy alternatives, see Guy Hunter, *The New Societies of Tropical
Africa*, and the very trenchant book by Reginald Green
and Ann Seidman, *Unity or Poverty? The Economics
of Pan-Africanism*.

On the liberation struggle in southern Africa, the
literature is growing at a fast pace. As starters, I
recommend Mary Benson, *South Africa, the Struggle for
a Birthright;* Amilcar Cabral, *Revolution in Guinea;*
Gerard Chaliand, *Armed Struggle in Africa;* Basil Davidson, *The Liberation of Guiné;* Ruth First, *South West
Africa;* and Eduardo Mondlane, *The Struggle for
Mozambique*.

African leaders themselves have not been shy about
publishing. Among others available in English, often in
more than one book, are, in alphabetical order: Obafemi
Awolowo, Nnamdi Azikiwe, Kofi Busia, Mamadou Dia,
Kenneth Kaunda, Jomo Kenyatta, Patrice Lumumba,
Tom Mboya, Kwame Nkrumah, Julius Nyerere, Léopold
Senghor and Sékou Touré. And of course the whole
corpus of Frantz Fanon's writings is by now well known.

Old fashioned ethnography is no longer in style. But
there are some good overviews by anthropologists which
talk of things traditional within the context of modern
change. I would suggest Georges Balandier, *Ambiguous
Africa;* Paul Bohannon, *Africa and the Africans;* Mel-
ville Herskovits, *The Human Factor in Changing Africa*
and Peter Lloyd, *Africa in Social Change*.

The African cultural renaissance is thriving. Novels,
poems and plays come out abundantly. One fountain-
head remains: *Présence Africaine* in Paris—a journal
and a publishing house. The writings of such men as
Chinna Achebe, Cheikh Hamidou Kane, Ezekiel

Mphahlele, James Ngugi, Abioseh Nicol, Ferdinand Oyono, Ousmane Sembene (also films), and Wole Soyinka are now well known even to many not especially interested in Africa. A collection like *Africa in Prose*, edited by O. R. Dathorne and Willfried Feuser, or *Modern Poetry from Africa*, edited by Ulli Beier and Gerald Moore, will give an entrée to prose and poetry respectively. Wilfred Cartey's *Whispers from a Continent* is a fascinating look at this literature from the inside.

INDEX

Abbas, Ferhat, 50, 98
Abbas, Mekki, 127
Abd-el-Kader, 122
Abidjan, 119
Africanus, Leo, 15
Algeria, 30, 39, 49, 50, 57, 58, 60, 67, 72, 73, 76, 77, 98, 110–111, 118, 122, 123, 150
Ali, Sonni, 18
Almoravids, 16
Anglo-Egyptian Sudan. *See* Sudan.
Angola, 30, 51, 68, 117
Ashanti, 19, 88, 127
Askia the Great, 18
Awolowo, Chief Obafemi, 47, 100, 127
Azanians, 21–22
Azikiwe, Nnamdi, 98, 100, 143

Balmer, Rev. W. T., 128–129
Bamun, 19
Barbary States, 143
Barotseland, 41
Basutoland, 109, 110
Battuta, Ibn, 15

Bechuanaland, 109
Belgian Congo, 51, 60, 144. *See also* Congo.
Belgium, 41, 60, 63, 67–68, 76–77, 111, 113, 138
Ben Barka, Mehdi, 93
Ben Bella, Ahmed, 57
Benin, 19
Biobaku, S. O., 126, 134
Boganda, Abbé Barthélemy, 100, 117
Bokar, Tierno, 131
Bourguiba, Habib, 98, 100, 110, 127
Brandenburg, 29
Brazil, 147
Brazzaville, 119
Britain. *See* England.
British Cameroons, 116
British East Africa, 107, 108
British Somaliland, 110, 112
British South Africa Company, 23
British West Africa, 60, 66, 67, 71, 107
Buganda, 41
Burma, 57
Bushmen, 24
Busia, K. A., 126

Cameron, Sir Donald, 41, 66
Cameroun (Formerly French Cameroons), 58, 66, 70 fn., 72, 78, 92, 95, 111, 116, 117, 118, 141 fn., 155, 158
Cape Colony, 30
Carthage, 14
Casablanca, 119
Central Africa Federation, 108
Central African Republic, 92, 97, 100, 158
Césaire, Aimé, 131
Ceylon, 57, 70, 147
Chad, 14, 14 fn., 77, 156, 158
Chaka (Zulu king), 122
Chilembwe, John, 143
China, 20, 21, 146–147, 150
Congo, 19, 23, 32, 38, 61, 67–68, 77, 88, 94, 95, 96, 98, 113, 114, 117, 119, 138, 143. See also Belgian Congo.
Congo (Brazzaville), 60, 98
Congo (Leopoldville). See Congo.
Conseil de l'Entente, 108, 116
Cordoba, 17
Cuba, 147

Dahomey, 19, 38, 78, 108, 140, 156, 157
de Gaulle, Charles, 71
Denmark, 29
Dia, Mamadou, 134
Diagne, Blaise, 104
Diallo, Abdoulaye, 114
Dike, K. O., 126
Diop, Alioune, 131
Diop, Cheikh Anta, 126, 129–130, 132, 134
Djenné, 17

Dogon, 25
Du Bois, W. E. B., 104, 130 fn., 143

Egypt, 12, 13, 70 fn., 129, 130, 138 fn., 139, 150
England, 29, 30, 41, 57, 60, 63, 64–65, 66, 68–70, 73–76, 89, 110, 111, 112, 113, 138, 144, 145, 156
Eritrea, 116
Ethiopia, 5, 21, 30, 110, 116, 146 fn.

Ferry, Jules, 65
Fezzan, 14
France, 29, 30, 40, 41, 49, 60, 63, 65–67, 70–76, 89, 110–111, 113, 138, 139, 145, 155 fn., 156
French Congo. See Congo (Brazzaville).
French Equatorial Africa, 51, 70 fn., 73 fn., 74, 77, 88, 111, 116–117
French North Africa, 33, 51, 72, 107, 150
French West Africa, 39, 57, 60, 67, 70 fn., 73 fn., 74, 88, 107, 108, 111, 114, 115, 116, 117, 150

Gabon (Gaboon), 30, 77, 88, 138, 155, 157, 160
Gaboon, 30
Gambia, 30, 41, 117
Gandhi, Mohandas Karamchand (Mahatma), 57

Gao, 18
Garamantes, 14
Germany, 63, 141 fn., 145
Ghana, Empire of, 16–17, 22,
   128
Ghana, Republic of (*also*
   Gold Coast), 17, 29, 30, 39,
   41, 56, 57, 64, 70, 72, 73,
   74, 76, 78, 86, 88, 90, 91,
   95, 97, 98, 100, 104, 107,
   108, 114, 117, 118, 126,
   128–129, 138, 138 fn., 141,
   141 fn., 143, 145, 155, 156,
   158, 159, 160
Gold Coast. *See* Ghana.
Great Zimbabwe, 22
Griaule, Marcel, 131
Guinea (formerly French
   Guinea), 38, 77, 86, 90,
   92, 95, 97, 98, 108, 114,
   117, 134, 138, 138 fn., 139,
   145, 150, 156, 159

Hadj, Messali, 55, 98
Hampaté, Amadou Ba, 131
Henrique, Bishop, 29
Hobhouse, Leonard T., 46
Holland, 29, 30
Houphouet-Boigny, Félix, 98,
   100, 101

Idrisi, al- (abu-'Abdullāh Mu-
   hammad ibn-Muhammad),
   20
India, 20, 23, 56, 57, 70, 147
Indian Ocean, 20, 22, 23
Indochina, 57, 72
Indonesia, 57, 147
Israel, 145–146

Italian Somaliland, 110
Italy, 6, 30, 72, 138
Ivory Coast, 39, 58, 77, 78,
   88, 95, 97, 98, 100, 108,
   118, 138, 141 fn., 156, 159

Japan, 147

Kasavubu, Joseph, 113 fn.
Katanga, 88
Kati, Mahmoud, 15
Keita, Modibo, 98
Keita, Sundiata, 17
Kenya, 21, 33, 39, 51, 55, 58,
   67, 69, 78, 100, 108, 110,
   116
Kenyatta, Jomo, 100, 104, 122
Ki Zerbo, Joseph, 126
Kushites, 13

Lagos, 30
Lebret, Father F. J., 148
Leopold I, King, 67, 143
Liberia, 5, 30, 32 fn., 103, 143
Libya, 6, 14, 72, 138, 139
Lugard, Lord Frederick, 41,
   64, 66
Ly Abdoulaye, 126
Lyautey, Marshal Louis, 66

Madagascar, 58, 73 fn., 132,
   138, 150 fn.
Maghreb, 110
Malagasy Republic, 49, 133
Mali, Empire of, 16, 17,
   129 fn.
Mali, Federation of, 108, 116,
   117

Mali, Republic of, 14 fn., 25, 77, 91, 95, 97, 98, 116, 117 fn., 129 fn., 131, 138, 138 fn., 150, 156, 158, 159
Malinowski, Bronislaw, 122
Mao Tse-tung, 146
Mapungubwe, 22, 23
Masudi, al- (Abu-al-Hasan 'Ali), 20
Mau Mau, 123, 125
Mauritania, 14 fn., 32 fn., 35, 157, 158
Melle. See Mali, Empire of.
Meroë, 13–14, 22
Mesopotamia, 20
Mexico, 147
Morocco, 15, 16, 18, 22, 41, 55, 66, 72, 73, 76, 78, 89, 93, 95, 96, 110–111, 139, 143, 150, 158
Mounier, Emmanuel, 148
Mozambique, 22, 30, 51, 68
Mphalehle, Ezekiel, 133 fn.
Munabbeh, Wahb Ibn, 15
Musa, Emperor Mansa, 17, 18

Netherlands, 57. See also Holland.
Niger, 14 fn., 92, 97, 108, 155, 156, 158, 159
Nigeria, 14, 14 fn., 19, 38, 39, 47, 56, 61, 64, 66, 70, 74, 76, 78, 86, 88, 89, 91, 95, 98, 100, 108, 112, 118, 126, 138, 140, 141 fn., 144, 159
Nketsia IV, Nana Kobina, 126
Nkrumah, Kwame, 98, 100, 101, 104, 114, 127, 143

Northern Rhodesia. See Rhodesia, Northern.
Nyasaland, 106, 108, 143
Nyerere, Julius, 98, 100, 109, 111, 134

Olympio, Sylvanus, 98
Oyo, 19

Padmore, George, 104, 114
Pakistan, 57, 70
Pléven, René, 71
Portugal, 29, 30, 63, 67, 68, 77
Portuguese Guinea, 30
Prester John, 21

Rabemananjara, Jacques, 133
Rhodes, Cecil, 49
Rhodesia, 22
    Northern, 32, 41, 143
    Southern, 33, 39, 69, 109
Ruanda-Urundi, 41
Russia, 46, 56, 143, 146, 150, 166

Sadi, Abderrahman es, 15
Sahara, 14, 17, 32 fn.
Salazar, Antonio de Oliveira, 68
Samory (Mandingo chief), 19, 122
Saõ Tomé e Principe, 30
Sartre, Jean-Paul, 133
Senegal, 30, 49, 51, 55, 56, 57, 65, 71, 88, 89, 92, 98, 100, 104, 117, 126, 131, 134, 138, 158, 159

Senegambia, 117

Senghor, Léopold-Sédar, 65, 88, 98, 100, 131, 132

Sheba, Queen of, 21

Sierra Leone, 30, 38, 41, 57, 90, 95, 103, 108, 138, 156

Solomon, King, 21

Somalia, 95, 110, 112, 122, 138, 150 fn.

Somaliland,
　British, 110, 112
　French, 73 fn., 110, 111
　Italian, 110

Songhay, 16, 17–19, 22

South Africa, Republic of, 6, 33, 33 fn., 51, 55, 58, 68, 69, 76, 109–110, 114 fn., 143, 150

Southern Rhodesia. *See* Rhodesia, Southern.

South-West Africa, 109–110

Soviet Union. *See* Russia.

Spain, 14

Stanley, Henry, 143

Sudan, 13, 39, 70 fn., 95, 96, 138, 139, 150 fn., 155, 158

Swaziland, 109

Sweden, 29

Tanganyika, 39, 41, 66, 97, 98, 109, 134

Tassili Mountains, 14

Tempels, Father Placide, 130–131

Timbuktu, 15, 16, 17, 18

Togo, 70 fn., 72, 73, 78, 90, 92, 95, 97, 98, 111, 138, 156, 157, 158

Touré, Sékou, 98, 134, 149, 150

Transvaal, 22, 32

Tunisia, 14, 55, 56, 72, 73, 78, 91, 95, 97, 98, 110–111, 116, 138, 139, 141, 150, 159

Uganda, 38, 39, 41, 78, 109, 118

Union of South Africa. *See* South Africa, Republic of.

United Arab Republic, 118, 158

United Kingdom. *See* England.

United Nations, 73, 109, 110, 114

United States, 56, 89, 143–145, 155 fn., 166

Upper Volta, 14 fn., 66, 95, 100, 108, 126, 155, 156, 158

Vandals, 15

Western Sudan, 13–19

Yaméogo, Maurice, 100

Yaoundé, 119

Youlou, Abbé Fulbert, 98, 101

Zanzibar, 41

Zimbabwe, 22–23

IMMANUEL WALLERSTEIN is a Professor of Sociology at McGill University. He has traveled extensively in Africa over a number of years. He has also published *Africa: The Politics of Unity* and *The Road to Independence: Ghana and the Ivory Coast*, as well as many articles on Africa in various journals including *Africa Report, Africa Today, Cahiers d'Etudes, Africaines, Etudes Congolaises, Journal of Modern African Studies*, and *Presence Africaine.*